Readers Praise *BACKWARDS:*
Returning to Our Source for Answers

"It is a book filled with breathtaking new insights and mind-expanding revelations. This book resonated with everything inside me that I think of as "me" and then went beyond to touch who I really am and that is a Being of Light. . . . After reading this I have gone beyond just hoping that what other near-death experiencers have told us is true to actually believing that what Nanci saw and heard is the true reality. This book takes the FEAR out of life."— Linda Hess, Charlottesville, VA

"There are any number of reports of people's near-death or out-of-body experiences, but few come back with much more of a message than that death is not to be feared, and God is love. . . . Nanci's personal experience is one of the few that tells us so much more, giving us a perspective that can truly change our lives, and our sense of purpose and direction. . . .[*BACKWARDS*] is highly readable, non-sensationalist (considering the subject), and Nanci makes valid comparisons with other well-respected publications in the field. Well worth reading to round out your understanding of life issues."–Anita P, Nurse, Australia

BACKWARDS is "the Rosetta Stone" of near-death experience books.–Hugh Wood, JD, Atlanta, Georgia.

"Through following countless near death accounts, I know yours is the most amazing, credible and awe-inspiring story. The Universal Knowledge you share rings true in my heart."—Chris Potter, Athens, TX

"The love and empathy that her writing exudes, yet as a trial lawyer by profession, makes this a read that I found hard to put down. It seems that her information is her life's experience now, and hits home with clarity of simplicity, as well as heart-felt, intuitive truth.

We get a female-feeling-tones version of this experience, which seems to balance so much information that is coming through the male dimension."– Gregory T. Pace, Columbus, Ohio

"I am certain that some folks will find many ideas strange, even controversial, and for good reason. Nanci doesn't mince words, but 'tells it like it is,' referencing her own deep NDE. . . . Challenging, intensely satisfying, thought provoking and ultimately affirming of our magnificence, we are then launched forward with the mission to bring this awareness of Love into our human life experience by attention and intention!"– Chip Eggerton, RN, Bradenton, Florida

"Have you ever read a book you bought thinking you'd get some spiritual structure, some explanation of just how to evolve through its pages, only to discover it talked in circles taking you nowhere? Well, throw those old books away, because *BACKWARDS: Returning to Our Source for Answers* will not spin a sugary tale, then lead to frustration like all those others; it will tell you where you're going and not only draw you a road map, but tell you how to take each step."–Sharon Wells, N. Hollywood, CA

"Due to and thanks to you and your book I am sure that my view on life and people has changed and will never be the same."–Ralf Klatt, Germany

"Her book comes alive for me, broadens new areas to pursue and excites me and gives me meaning. . . [T]his near-death book is very, very different from any others I have read."–Irene Osher, Long Island, NY

BACKWARDS
GUIDEBOOK

Also by Nanci L. Danison

BACKWARDS: Returning to Our Source for Answers

BACKWARDS: Returning to Our Source for Answers (6-CD
audiobook edition)

Light Answers to Tough Questions: A Primer on Life and Death (CD)

Light Answers to Tough Questions: What Happens When We Die? (CD)

Light Answers to Tough Questions: What is God? What are we? (2 CDs)

BACKWARDS

GUIDEBOOK

A Companion to BACKWARDS: Returning to Our
Source for Answers

Nanci L. Danison

A.P. Lee & Co., Ltd., Publishers
Columbus, OH

Printed in Canada by Friesens, Inc.

AP Lee & Co., Ltd., Publishers
PO Box 340292
Columbus, OH 43234
"Evolving mankind, one book at a time."

Cover design: Gwyn Kennedy Snider
Cover photo: Bernat Armangue, Associated Press. Words of comfort lining the interior membrane of the 35-foot glass tower of the Atocha Memorial, Madrid, Spain. Licensed for use by AP/WIDE WORLD PHOTOS.

Reprinted with the permission of ATRIA BOOKS, an imprint of Simon & Schuster Adult Publishing Group from WHAT GOD WANTS by Neale Donald Walsch. Copyright © 2005 by Neale Donald Walsch. From CONVERSATIONS WITH GOD: AN UNCOMMON DIALOGUE, BOOK 1 by Neale Donald Walsch, copyright © 1995 by Neale Donald Walsch. Used by permission of G.P. Putnam's Sons, a division of Penguin Group (USA) Inc. From FOCUSING by Dr. Eugene T. Gendlin, copyright © 1978, 1981 by Eugene T. Gendlin, Ph.D. Used by permission of Bantam Books, a division of Random House, Inc. Reprinted with the permission of The Free Press, a Division of Simon & Schuster, Inc. from YOU: Staying Young: The Owner's Manual for Extending Your Warranty Michael F. Roizen, MD and Mehmet C. Oz, MD. Copyright © 2007 by Michael F. Roizen, MD and Oz Works LLC. All rights reserved.

The author of this book does not dispense psychological or spiritual advice or prescribe the use of any technique as a form of treatment for physical or medical problems without the advice of a physician, either directly or indirectly. The intent of the author is only to offer information of a general nature to help you in your quest for well being. In the event you use any of the information in this book for yourself, the author and the publisher shall have no responsibility for any loss or damage caused, or alleged to have been caused, directly or indirectly, by the information contained in this book.

Library of Congress Control Number: 2008932657
ISBN-13: 978-1-934482-02-5
ISBN-10: 1-934482-02-1

Contents

CONTENTS

Preface

BACKWARDS: RETURNING TO OUR *Source for Answers* was published in October 2007, after a work effort that took eleven years. The original manuscript totaled over 700 pages when formatted into book form. Obviously, the publisher asked me to edit it down to a readable length. I did that by removing the question and answer sections, some examples, and other explanatory material. Much of that original material fills this book. Some of it will appear in subsequent books. Of necessity, some passages in this book repeat concepts from the first book for clarity and completeness.

I have summarized my beyond death experience in Chapter 14 to provide background for readers who have not read the first book in the *BACKWARDS* series. Some of this material had been deleted from the first book and so does not duplicate Chapters 20-22 of *BACKWARDS*. Both descriptions should be read to get the full chronology of events.

June 26, 2008

Acknowledgments

Too many people have assisted in the publication of this book for me to thank them each personally here. I have tried to thank each one for his/her contribution at the time it was given. I apologize if I have missed one of you. I especially want to thank the readers who have written to me with questions. I hope each of you wonderful Light Beings knows how much your support sustains me.

Some of the talented people who have helped produce this second book include: Sydney Long, always my first editor; my editors Beth Rubin and Loraine Stout; Gwyn Kennedy Snider, who designed the book cover; and my friends and family at A.P. Lee & Co., Ltd., who never fail to support me. A special thanks is extended to the authors and publishers who have allowed me to weave their innovative thoughts and words into my text as validation of my own personal experience.

BACKWARDS

GUIDEBOOK

A Companion to BACKWARDS: Returning to Our
Source for Answers

Part I – We Have It Backwards

The first part of *BACKWARDS: Returning to Our Source for Answers* expresses memories from when I searched Universal Knowledge during my afterlife experience for the answers to life's most important questions: What is God? What am I? What does God expect of me? What is the purpose of life? Where is heaven? Where is hell? What is the true religion?

Part I of this *Guidebook* expands on three of these topics: the nature of God, our true spiritual nature, and the purpose of undertaking human life.

Chapter 1 provides an overview of the major spiritual concepts discussed in both books to set the stage for those who have not read the first volume of this two-volume set.

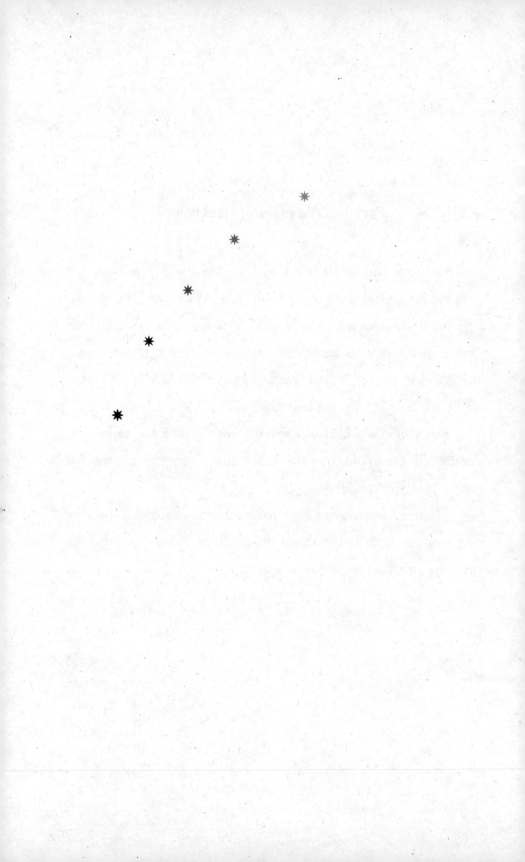

I

* Backwards View

IN *BACKWARDS: RETURNING TO Our Source for Answers,* I shared that I had discovered in the midst of an extensive afterlife experience that many of our most firmly held beliefs about life and death are backwards.

I was shocked to learn that souls are completely different beings than the human animals they inhabit. Souls, the spirits who enter the afterlife after humans die, are not themselves human. Nor are they part of human beings. Humans are animals native to Earth that have their own life force, personalities, and innate character traits. Humans have no souls.

I personally observed and experienced that souls are entirely spiritual beings that near-death survivors call Beings of Light. Others might call them angels or guides. Souls have their own life force, personalities, and innate character traits that are different from humans'. Souls have no bodies.

I was shown that WE are souls, not humans. We silently inhabit human animals but are not part of them.

I include "backwards" in my book titles to highlight how our human societies reinforce the erroneous assumption that we are human beings, rather than separate spiritual beings who inhabit human bodies. Our collective perspective has traditionally been limited to what a human comprehends. Even our religious belief systems are based on human nature, instead of our true spiritual nature. This causes us to look backwards—backwards to a lower level of being for our understanding of life and death. And it results in errors in our belief systems.

For example, many of us assume the human way of life continues after death. The afterlife, we are told by religions, is a more glorified version of human existence, only lived in God's presence. The afterlife I lived bore no resemblance to Earth life.

Our use of human life as the template for eternity leads to the erroneous belief that life after death will transpire in a shared physical environment—like our Earthly experience where we all see the same land, sea, and sky. Heaven is often described as crystal cities, golden streets, and mansions for all. We ignore the fact that a spiritual environment has no physical matter, which would be needed to mimic these Earthly settings.

Similarly, many religions share a "resurrection of the dead" concept. Their followers believe decayed human bodies will be reconstituted, glorified, and rejoined with their souls in heaven after the end of the world. No one explains how a spiritual, non-physical dimension can support the weight of human bodies, or why we would want them with their limited abilities.

It is very human to arrogantly project human expectations onto the entire universe, even the afterlife. Humans are self-absorbed by nature. They cannot rise above it. But WE can. And we must. It is time to adopt belief systems based on a higher level of perspective: the spiritual level—our own true nature.

There are some commonalities, some unequivocal truths about the universe that we all remember as we transition from human life to spirit. Unfortunately, we cannot remember them while in the flesh unless we make an effort to do so. That is why spiritual truths do not automatically hold the prominent place in our hearts they deserve.

BACKWARDS: Returning to Our Source for Answers lays out the *spiritual* facts of life and death, as I understood them during my exposure to Universal Knowledge while I was dead. Life and death are amazingly simple from the spiritual vantage point. I chose to return to physical life to bring this perspective forward, and to show how spiritual truths differ from human beliefs. Some of those differences explored in the *BACKWARDS* books are:

> Some religions portray their deity as a human father figure. The god I experienced firsthand is neither male nor human-like. It is the source of our universe and should not be denigrated as a mere human father figure. What I call "Source" is what most religions refer to as the one supreme deity. Source is an enormous, self-aware, all-knowing, and omnipresent Energy field.

Its nature is more analogous to electricity, or raw energy, than to human nature. And Source's form is closer to an "entity" than a being.

Many of us believe Source is separate from us and exists "up there" somewhere. Source is not separate from us. It is a Collective Being *composed* of all of us and of all of creation. Source is not now, and never has been, separated from us. We are one and the same. We are literally part of Source, with the same innate characteristics, including curiosity, creativity, multiple levels of awareness, total knowledge, ability to manifest reality, and unconditionally loving nature (described in detail in Chapter 3 of *BACKWARDS: Returning to Our Source for Answers*).

We believe Source to be a supervisory figure that controls everything that happens in our daily lives. In fact, Source gave us complete control over what we experience. We choose what happens in our lives, either consciously or unconsciously. We truly have free will. Source does not have a prescribed plan for our lives. We create our own individual journeys as we evolve back to Source.

Many of us believe the soul is part of what we are as human beings. We are NOT human beings. We are actually powerful Beings of Light—extensions of Source's self-awareness—who have chosen to inhabit human animals. Humans, and the Light Beings we call "souls," are two different beings. Each has its own personality, emotions, beliefs, and innate nature. We are the Light Beings inside the humans.

We believe we are separate from each other, and, therefore, that our actions have no consequences beyond our own lives. The truth is: we all collectively constitute one entity—Source. We are all interconnected within Source. Because of this, everything we do affects everyone else, and Source itself to some degree. We are responsible to everyone else for the consequences of our actions. Accepting this responsibility, and choosing to act from unconditional love, will open us up to our true spiritual nature.

We believe our thoughts are private, inconsequential, and have no power unless we act them out. To the contrary, our thoughts *are* power. The power of our "attention and intention" manifests reality, as humans understand that term. And, because we co-create reality with others, our thoughts impact the lives of those around us. Each of us is responsible for our share of co-creating all the evils in this world. To improve human living conditions, we must learn to manifest consciously from love rather than unconsciously from fear.

We fear death and the end of physical existence. But death does not end *our* lives because *we are not physical.* Only the human animal hosts die. Their fear of death is what we feel. Our hosts' deaths release us to awaken to our full Light Being state of expanded awareness, instant access to Universal Knowledge, wondrous abilities, and ecstasy in the Light of Source's love—a state we call the afterlife.

During merger with God (what I call Source), I was made to understand that we are extensions of Source's own consciousness. We are literally part of Source. The significance of this revelation is that we are not limited to the physical abilities human bodies possess. We have tremendous Source-given power to improve our lives and our world. We need only to access it.

It may not be easy to embrace new spiritual truths here on Earth, no matter how much they may resonate within us. We have lived many years (and lives) in the shadow of human-created truths—fear-based beliefs deeply rooted in superstition and ancient mythologies. But the effort to change our belief systems to be more in line with our spiritual nature will be its own reward. It will allow us to develop awareness of our eternal selves, our Light Being selves, and to consciously access our spiritual powers.

Awakening to our true nature as facets of Source's consciousness may require a shift in perspective from human to divine.

We have all changed perspectives before. Six-year-old children view the world far differently than their parents do. Students think their lives are hard until they encounter the greater stresses of the working world. Everyone's view of life changes with time because of increased experience. And the more experience we gain, the greater level of understanding we have from viewing an event within a larger context.

Do not be concerned if this book triggers feelings of resistance, or even rejection. That is the human host's response to new ideas. Humans fight change because of innate self-preservation instincts. Preserving the way things are now, maintaining the status quo, feels like preserving the self to the human animal. We need to recognize and accept that about our hosts.

Some people spend their whole lives trying to maintain the status quo. They fight growth with their full emotional and physical arsenal. For example, the newspapers recently carried a photo of a small house and lot surrounded on three sides by a tall concrete commercial building that occupied the rest of the block. The story highlighted the owner's adamant refusal to sell the property to the developer of the commercial building. There is nothing wrong with holding fast to one's homestead. But, under these circumstances, it does signal a reluctance to accept change.

It is ironic that our human hosts instinctively dodge change in their lives. Believing change can be avoided is a cosmic joke. The human body changes on the cellular level every day. Every few days the esophagus has a new lining. Every five days new liver cells generate. Stool is brown because old red blood cells are being sloughed off as they are replaced.[1] We do not inhabit the same bodies now that we did thirty years ago.

Some of us may adopt human behavior and resist changing our beliefs for an entire human lifetime. That effort is futile. We will simply be born again into new bodies, and the struggle against growth will begin anew. Our reincarnation may go on for three, thirty, or three hundred human lifetimes, until we finally realize that we need change to evolve. We might as well tape a note to our refrigerator doors right now that says "I love change," and read it every day, because just making that one seemingly small attitude adjustment can improve our lives immeasurably. Just think of what a difference it would make to be able to face change and feel joy rather than fear. To feel child-like excitement, wonder, and anticipation; instead of grief, loss, and dread.

This *Guidebook* is designed to help you make a transition in thinking and believing from the prevalent human perspective to a spiritual one. The concepts may sound alien at first. But they are ultimately far simpler than the philosophies and faiths with which we are so familiar.

Throughout the ages we have been told that the reality of heaven and the afterlife is incomprehensible to man. As a result, nearly all religious and spiritual writings speak in metaphor, in an attempt to provide a watered-down human perspective explanation of these divine "mysteries." For example, heaven has been characterized as a physical environment, like Earth, because that is understandable to humans. Source is portrayed as a rule-maker because our creator has been cast in the role of a human parent. Author Kurt Leland paints a graphic picture of how unfamiliar images and concepts from the afterlife translate in our minds into familiar ones:

> Imagine what it would be like to find yourself suddenly transported to ancient China. You don't know the language, the alphabet, or the customs. Once culture shock has worn off, you may begin to notice that ancient Chinese society has a highly sophisticated, though alien, structure. Through comparing this structure with the one you're used to, you can make deductions about appropriate behavior. You're setting up a mental *translation table*. For example, you may suddenly realize that a formerly obscure gesture functions as a ritual form of greeting and necessitates a certain response—just as the offer of a hand leads to a handshake today.
>
> As a prospective explorer of nonphysical reality, you'll be in much the same position. Unless you make a translation table by comparing your experiences in nonphysical reality with your experiences in physical reality, there's little hope that you'll ever make sense of what you perceive there.[2]

The *BACKWARDS* series of books provide a translation table for understanding the constructs of life, death, and the afterlife from a purely spiritual perspective.

It is time to bring our medieval belief systems into the twenty-first century. Our lives today are filled with sophisticated concepts, not only from medicine and science, but also supplied by the science fiction in which we are all immersed through books, TV, virtual reality games, and graphic novels. We routinely grasp notions founded on quantum physics, microbiology, and aerospace technology. We have a far-ranging translation table today that was unavailable to historic writers. The *BACKWARDS* books use language more up-to-date than our ancient texts to make the context more familiar. Using updated language renders the realities of Source, the afterlife, and our own true nature no longer incomprehensible.

❋   ❋   ❋

This *Guidebook* describes the major premises found in *BACKWARDS: Returning to Our Source for Answers* from three different perspectives: the human animal's viewpoint, the Light Being's vantage point, and Source's ultimate comprehension. Comparisons are made to highlight how limited our understanding of universal truths can be while we occupy these bodies, and to help expand our thinking.

Parts of this *Guidebook* take the form of questions and answers. Some of the questions simply draw out the fact that we already believe many of the truths set forth in *BACKWARDS: Returning to Our Source for Answers*, though we may have been characterizing them differently in our minds. The discussions after the questions seek to gently guide us from current belief systems to one more in line with our own true nature as Beings of Light. The questions, answers, and exercises help translate what I learned firsthand about life, death, and the afterlife into today's terminology.

The mental exercises in this book may not fulfill anyone's criterion for logic. Logic was not my goal. Rather, my hope is that something in these pages will trigger spontaneous "knowings" for you. Will trigger access to Universal Knowledge to answer all your questions and resolve all your doubts.

2
What Is God?

MY OWN HIGHER POWER turned out to be literally that—an immensely powerful living Energy Source. When I died in 1994, I came face-to-face, so to speak, with the entity we call God, and I now call Source. The encounter was not at all what I expected.

Instead of an immensely powerful *person*, Source revealed itself to be the Energy creating and maintaining the universe. Our whole universe, and everything in it, is part and parcel of one supreme deity. So, to the extent that it is a being, Source would have to be described as a "collective being," for Source includes within it every other being that exists. Merger into Source near the end of my afterlife adventure dispelled any illusion I ever had of a divine presence that is a singular being.

The differences between how humans typically perceive Source, and what I experienced, may be summarized in the following table:

Human Perspective	Light Being Perspective	Source's Perspective
God is a separate being from me. He created me as a human being.	I am part of Source. Source created me as a spiritual being.	All "beings" in the universe are facets of my own personality.

Most religions do not describe a Supreme *Being* as its deity anyway. Rather, their doctrines and catechisms revolve around a type of Super*man*.

Our religions describe a Creator who acts just like some humans do—a father figure, but with questionable emotional stability. The supreme being is kind and loving one day, granting us blessings. The next day, this same deity is a vengeful creature micromanaging our daily lives, demanding our adherence to antiquated rules if we are to avoid eternal punishment in a fiery hell. The deity of many religions demands wars, terrorism, and atrocities the likes of which would make the most violent videogame characters blush. In other words, a divinity that acts out the worst human traits.

Let us examine our beliefs about our god's character traits to see whether "he" is, or is not, like humans.

✳   ✳   ✳

Question 1: Do you believe in a deity that is eternal?

Discussion: Many of us believe in a deity[3] that lives forever. Immortality is fundamental to our definition of a god. Our deity must have abilities beyond those of humans. Otherwise, why would we elevate him to a greater status than our own? So, our deity must exceed humans. Be superhuman. Yet, according to many religions, still act a lot like man. That would make the deity a Super*man*.

Anyone who knows the Superman comic book story understands that Kryptonite can kill the super hero. Not so immortal, him. But we know nothing can kill our supreme deity; for unlike man, he is truly immortal. But still, he is emotionally very much like man, at least according to our belief systems.

Source is eternal and nothing like humans.

✳   ✳   ✳

Question 2: Do you believe in a deity that is all-powerful?

Discussion: Again, our very concept of a god requires him to be all-powerful. To have superhuman powers—even power over life and death, inasmuch as we agree our deity is immortal. Many religions teach that the deity can be, do, and have anything and everything he desires. He created this entire universe. And he can end it if he chooses. Unlike man, the deity has all the power we can imagine. But, he uses that power very much like we would, or so we believe.

Source is all-powerful and created the universe. It does not wield its power as humans would.

*　　*　　*

Question 3: Do you believe in a deity that is all knowing?

Discussion: Many religions profess that the one highest god knows all. He knows everything that ever was or that ever will be known in the universe. He has unlimited access to the past, present, and future. He knows our deepest thoughts and desires. Nothing in creation can be hidden from this deity. But, he uses that knowledge against us, to foil our happiness, if we do not act as religion dictates.

Source is all knowing and does not use it against us.

*　　*　　*

Question 4: Do you believe in a deity that is present everywhere in our universe and beyond?

Discussion: I was taught that God is present everywhere, in all things, and in all people. There is nowhere in our universe off limits to the deity. He is omni-present.

Nevertheless, many religions stress that we are totally separate beings from god. We are taught the deity is our father, and we are his children. We all know human children are separate beings from their parents. So this analogy creates the same impression of separation. Never was I told before dying that I am literally *part of* the entity I grew up calling "God."

Source is the only entity present in our universe. All of creation constitutes Source.

✳ ✳ ✳

Question 5: Do you believe in a deity that sees everything you do? Sees all that goes on in our world?

Discussion: If you believe the deity is omnipresent, then you must assume he sees everything as well. We generally do not envision a blind god. Nor do we suspect he pays no attention to where he is, including everywhere. True, we may assume he's too busy from time to time to answer our prayers, but that is not because he cannot see our needs. The supreme being sees all. He just seems to ignore us sometimes, like a human might.

Source is aware of everything in the universe.

✳ ✳ ✳

Question 6: Do you believe in a deity that loves you "unconditionally," but will punish you if you break his laws?

Discussion: Most religions include the premise that the deity has rules or laws that humans must follow in order to enter into heaven or attain paradise. This is much like the rules our parents set for us as we grew up in their households. We are told that certain actions are sins, the performance of some of which will condemn us to everlasting damnation. Our parents likewise set certain limits, which if exceeded could have gotten us thrown out of their homes. Thus, our deity seems to behave as a human parent might.

Does a deity who cannot die; created the universe; can be, do, and have anything he wants; knows all there is to know; is present everywhere all the time; and sees everything that goes on in our lives sound very human?

We collectively as the human race can envision a deity that is immortal, eternal, all-powerful, all knowing, omnipresent, and all seeing. But we cannot imagine that same deity being all loving because humans are not? God cannot accept us exactly as we are regardless of what we do and must punish us for transgressions? Well, perhaps the deity of our current understanding cannot.

But the Source I met can—and loves us no matter what we do.

We must change our historical understanding of a deity to be able to accept that the same being that exceeds human abilities and capacities on every other front, also exceeds the human capacity to love. Source is NOT like humans in that regard, and never has been. Our Source loves us *unconditionally*. No strings attached. There are no prerequisites for that love, not even forgiveness for our sins. All we have to be is who we already are—literal extensions of Source itself.

Source has not handed down rules, etched on stone tablets or otherwise, that must be followed to earn its love. We cannot earn Source's love, or heaven, by being "good" any more than toes can earn a place on the foot by being useful. We are already *there* as parts of Source, just as toes are already firmly attached to feet. It is nature's design.

Why is this so hard to accept? Why must we cling to the delusion that the deity punishes us for breaking rules? Even condemns us to eternal suffering for so-called "mortal sins?"

Our religions draw us to such fear-based dogma by the millions. Why? *Because* of the fear. Because we fear what will happen if we do not believe. As one reader told me, "Nanci, if you are right, and I don't believe you, the worst thing that can happen to me is I will automatically return to Source." But, he adds, "if religion is right, and I don't believe it, the worst thing that can happen is I will be condemned to hell for all eternity. I think I'll hedge my bets and follow religion."

That logic is perfectly sound.

Who wants to challenge thousands of years of accepted faith? Accepted as fact, even, by the truly convinced.

Who? Anyone who wants the truth. Anyone who truly wants to know the unvarnished-by-human-imagination nature of Source.

Anyone who believes that he/she is more than flesh and bones. Anyone who has experienced the briefest moment of unconditional love and KNOWS it is Source's true nature. Anyone who is tired of fear running his or her life. Anyone who has noticed the conflict between what we believe about the deity's character in other respects, and what we believe of its capacity to love us.

We can all expand our understanding of our Creator from the limitations imposed by our current human experience to a more enlightened view as expressed below:

Human Perspective	Light Being Perspective	Source's Perspective
God sets rules that I must follow to earn Heaven.	I am an extension of Source's own self-awareness and am evolving back to Source automatically.	My thought-forms ("beings") have never left my mind and so do not have to return to me. They are each cherished aspects of my own self-awareness.

*　　*　　*

Question 7: What would a deity that lives forever, and can have anything it wants forever and ever, want with us?

Discussion: Some religions provide a direct answer to this question. Others do not. The one I studied as a child taught me that the deity created man "to know God, to love God, and to serve God," or words to that effect. I do not recall ever being told that the reverse is likewise true: that God created me to know me, love me, and serve me. My church would have considered such a thought blasphemous.

Do we really believe that Source created us to know and love it but *not* vice versa?

Is it not possible that Source created us not for what we can do for it, but for the pure joy of creating US? The joy of knowing US? Loving US unconditionally, always? Experiencing US as we travel through physical and non-physical lives in worlds all over the universe? We are, after all, integral parts of Source. Do we believe Source does not love itself completely, fully, and unconditionally?

What does Source demand of us in return for its unconditional love? Nothing.

"You have just seen the answer to the most important question in human history," says Neale Donald Walsch in *What God Wants*.[4]

> What does God want?
> Nothing.
> *Absolutely nothing at all.*
> Please think about this. . . .

The relationship with God that so many people on Earth have established falls apart if it is true that God wants nothing at all from human beings. Yet that the relationship falls apart does not mean the relationship has ended. Sometimes things need to fall apart for things to truly fall together for the first time. It does not always serve us to shy away from ideas that may cause things to fall apart. So let's look again, and now more deeply, at this idea:

What does God want?

Nothing.

Absolutely nothing at all.[5]

Why should we believe this "nothing" theory when for millennia well-founded and accepted religious institutions have taught us differently? Personally, I do *not* believe it. I *know* it is true because I actually experienced it and have returned to tell you that truth.

Near the end of my beyond death experience I merged into the Source—not to the point of dissolving as an individual, but enough to have firsthand knowledge of its nature. The depth, breadth, richness, and vastness of Source's love are so far beyond human comprehension there literally are no words to describe it. The tenderness with which Source treated my desire to return to human life, to tell others about our true nature, has permanently touched my heart so profoundly that fourteen years later I still tear up remembering it. More importantly, though it was clear that Source had decided it was time for me to dissolve back into it, Source allowed me to return to human life just because I wanted to share what I had learned. Source asked nothing of me, not even that I accept the end of my human lifetime.

If Source wants nothing from us, why would we believe violation of any rule, or failure to worship or serve Source, would result in punishment? If nothing is expected of us, Source cannot be disappointed by what we choose to do. It would have no reason to impose punishment for actions taken or avoided.

Humankind has projected onto its deity the human emotions of expectation, disappointment, judgment, and desire for punishment. More importantly, humans have projected onto Source the unique human perspective that "there is no free lunch." Our host bodies have observed the cause and effect relationships prevalent in Earth life, and we believe it to be a universal constant. We even call it a scientific fact—the law of cause and effect.

We cannot conceive of a situation where there is no cause and effect, no tit for tat, no "you scratch my back and I'll scratch yours." The belief that nothing good is truly free is so ingrained in us that even our fictional superheroes are violent and vengeful. They act more like animals than superheroes. Authors, artists, and actors also attribute human violence to alien species in their works of fiction simply because violence is what we observe of man. We are collectively incapable of believing in true benevolence. Humans are suspicious of it.

We cannot accept that our own Creator could love us truly, and honestly, unconditionally, with no expectation of anything in return.

Ah, you say, but Source does get something in return: our experiences. *BACKWARDS: Returning to Our Source for Answers* tells us that Source created us in order to experience itself and the wonders of the universe it created. So, Source gets what it wants from us because "as souls, we literally serve as Source's arms and legs, to have physical experiences for Source. We are the body of Source. And, as its body, our job is to carry God/Source into everything we do."[6]

So, it is not true that Source wants nothing from us. That is correct. Source does want us to have experiences, in other words, to live. In return for giving us life, Source wants us to *live*. That is it. Just LIVE. With all that life entails. But *we* choose how we will live. And many of us do not do well in that regard. Then we blame Source for that.

Perhaps if we understood ourselves a little better, we might be more willing to accept that Source created us out of love simply to live. We might be able to accept the mental shift required to move from the human perspective to a true understanding of Source's love for us.

3

What Am I?

AT THE VERY BEGINNING of my afterlife adventure, I discovered that the person I had always believed myself to be is not my true identity. Think about it. Living outside the body I had once inhabited could not help but change my perspective on who I really am. My human identity was gone. Familiar human personality traits, like fear and the need for control, were drifting away. Entrenched beliefs about life and death crashed around me as I continued to *live* without breathing or heart beating. But the most astonishing realization was that I am not a human being at all.

What then am I?

As my thoughts turned to answering that question, what I call "knowings" about our true nature, and how it differs from human nature, inundated my mind. "Knowing" is the spiritual phenomenon of having a detailed and deep understanding of a topic suddenly appear in one's mind, accompanied by the conviction that the information is absolutely true. While experiencing "knowings," I *felt* I had known the truth forever, but had simply forgotten it while in human form.

As I sorted through the "knowings," I became keenly aware that most of my Earthly efforts had been spent on animal survival activities. I had devoted considerable time and energy to making sure my body was nourished and rested. Striving to make good grades in school, to achieve financial success at work, and to eventually gain recognition and respect from legal colleagues had consumed a large part of my life. "Knowings" made me understand that those endeavors were nothing more than animal competitiveness. They gained me nothing on a spiritual level. I was ashamed of the triviality of my life's efforts. None of my accomplishments mattered after death because not one of them survived loss of the human body.

Moving deeper through the transition to spiritual nature, I discovered that the human emotions so familiar to me are rudimentary compared to the heightened ones I enjoyed in the Light. The *types* of emotions are the same—except for the absence of fear—but the degree to which I experienced them changed radically. The comparison between the two is as dramatic as the difference in taste humans experience when they can, and cannot, smell their food. The tongue only senses sweet, salty, sour, and bitter. The nose brings the delightfulness of aroma to taste, giving humans a wealth of flavor sensations. In the Light, human emotions seemed more like the tongue's limited range of tastes as compared to the richness of seasonings contributed by the sense of smell.

Similarly, I found my sense of identity expanding exponentially the longer I remained in the Light. While in human life, I had believed myself to *be* human. Through an incremental transition process, I began to remember who and what I truly am. I am not human. I am part of Source. We all are.

The person I think of as myself is not actually the human being I see in the mirror. Personal experience gained by dying proved to me that what we perceive as one integrated human is actually two separate "beings," as humans use that term. One is a human animal destined for temporary Earth life. The other is an eternal non-physical Energy mass I call a Light Being. Part of the Light Being inhabits the human being as its "soul." After combining, each being still retains its own innate character traits and personality.

The most wonderful aspect of this dual being nature—human body infused with immortal Light Being soul—is the truth that we are not the animal part of the package. We are the immortal Light Being that does not die, cannot be physically injured, and enjoys the bliss of living in a heavenly state between physical lifetimes.

Amnesia of our true nature over the millennia has trapped us in a mindset that has put the emphasis on studying the wrong being. Developing the wrong character traits. Prizing the wrong personality. That is completely understandable. But it is backwards.

The time has come to put aside our ignorance and learn what has been revealed to us time and time again over the ages.

We are not human beings. Part of our Light Being Energy inhabits humans as a means of self-expression and lifestyle. The person we each see in our reflection is an animal indigenous to planet Earth who has been entrusted to our care as a physical host. He/she is the temple of our spirit, so to speak. We are not that animal. Not a human. We are the incredibly wonderful and powerful spiritual being *inside* the human animal.

How can you confirm this—without actually dying? This Chapter will ask several questions, experiments in perspective as it were, to help you decide for yourself who you really are.

✳   ✳   ✳

Question 1: Do you believe you have a soul?

Discussion: Whatever you may call it, most of us believe we have a soul or spirit that separates from the body upon its death and goes to heaven or paradise. Conventional thought is that the soul is one part of a human being, which itself is composed of two parts: body and soul. The "knowings" I gained in the Light taught me this is incorrect. Humans are purely physical beings with no spiritual component. What we call a "soul" is the Light Being Energy that inhabits the human body.

So, no, you do not have a soul. You *are* a soul.

* * *

Question 2: Do you believe that the soul *enters* the human's body sometime at or before birth and leaves it at death?

Discussion: Most belief systems readily acknowledge that the soul leaves the body at death. Ghosts are a prevalent feature in our art and literature and seem to intrigue most of us, regardless of religious background. Psychics and mediums abound in our world and are often consulted to communicate with souls who have "crossed over." So, it appears that many people believe the soul leaves the body at its death and continues to live in an afterlife.

A logical extension of this belief is that the soul must have entered the body at some point, in order to be able to leave it at death.

* * *

Question 3: Do you believe a soul is alive in and of itself? That it is alive independent of the body—like a being?

Discussion: Some religions teach that the soul brings life to the body. But medical science has proven that once sperm enters ovum, the combined fertilized egg will, of its own innate nature, begin to divide. And divide. And divide until an entire human being is formed. This happens not only in utero but also in a test tube. It would appear, then, that DNA is the life force that produces life in a human animal body. Many people do acknowledge that the DNA of other types of animals creates life. The same concept may not be as acceptable to us when applied to humans.

No religion teaches that when sperm penetrates egg the resulting combination of DNA creates the immortal soul. The souls in humans must come from something other than DNA.

Because most of us already believe that the soul enters into a human at or before birth, leaves the body at death, and thereafter lives joyously in heaven or paradise, we must believe it is capable of life. The soul must have its own life outside the human being. Like a being—a living being with its own life force. Most of us generally agree that the soul has no physical mass and is typically considered to be spirit. Would you agree that it is made mostly of energy? Might it even be an energy being? Is it so far-fetched now to believe that a Light or Energy Being enters into a human animal body to serve as its soul? Might you be that soul?

Question 4: If you, the soul, enter a body before birth, doesn't that mean you were alive *prior to* being infused into a human being?

Discussion: Most religions teach that the soul is immortal. It lives forever. Doesn't forever include the time before your current body was born? If you as soul were alive before becoming part of a human body, wouldn't that mean you have a life of your own apart from human life? In fact, you do. A very long and rich life.

Personally, before my beyond death experience, I thought my soul was created by God to be this one human being, Nanci. I believed my soul was infused into my body at birth, presumably directly from the hand of God. I had never heard of reincarnation in my religion and had never given it a thought as it pertains to my own life. One of the most explosive shocks that rocked my world when I died was the discovery that I had memories of having lived hundreds or thousands of lives in other human and non-human forms. I recalled the details of hundreds of lifetimes. Memories! How could I remember those lives if I had not lived them? And to have lived them, I would have had to exist long before the birth of Nanci. I saw with my own (spiritual) eyes that reincarnation is a fact for me. I was forced to accept that my physical existence has not been confined to this one human lifetime.

How we think of ourselves is simply habit. Habits can be broken, dramatically as I discovered, or through effort. Try the following exercise to see if it has an impact on how you view yourself.

✳   ✳   ✳

Exercise: Suppose you have met someone for the first time and know nothing about him or her, and vice versa, but you want to get acquainted. The stranger says to you, "Who are you? Tell me about yourself." What is your response?

Discussion: When someone asks us who we are, often we identify ourselves by the roles we perform in our work life. We may say, "I'm a computer programmer." Or, the answer may be: salesman, waiter, accountant, cashier, or the name of whatever else we spend the bulk of our time doing. I say, "I'm a lawyer" or "I'm a writer," depending upon who is asking and which role I think they will find more interesting. We all identify with what we do.

In responding to the question of who we are, some of us may mistakenly over-identify with our work and believe that designation sums us up as a person. "I am *just* a stay-at-home mom." "I am *just* a secretary." "I am *unemployed*." "I am a *doctor*." Notice how in our thinking we have attached a judgment to what we do for a living and thus have judged *ourselves*? Limited ourselves?

When we fall into the trap of thinking we *are* what we do—that our identity is bound up with our animal survival task of earning a living—we make a mistake. Who we truly are has nothing to do with what activities we choose to experience while in human form. The book *Conversations with God: An Uncommon Dialogue* presents God having a conversation with Neale Donald Walsch about . . . everything. In the following excerpt God explains why what we *do* does not define us.

> There's a difference between being and doing, and most people have placed their emphasis on the latter. . . .
>
> *Doing* is a function of the body. *Being* is a function of the soul. The body is always doing *something*. Every minute of

every day it's up to *something*. It never stops, it never rests, it's constantly *doing* something.

It's either doing what it's doing at the behest of the soul—or in spite of the soul. The quality of your life hangs in the balance.

The soul is forever *being*. It is being what it is being, regardless of what the body is doing, not *because* of what it's doing.

If you think your life is about doingness, you do not understand what you are about.

Your soul doesn't care *what* you do for a living—and when your life is over, neither will you. Your soul cares only about what you're *being* while you're doing *whatever* you're doing.

It is a state of beingness the soul is after, not a state of doingness.

What is the soul seeking to be?

Me.

You.

Yes, Me. Your soul *is* Me, and it knows it. What it is doing, is trying to *experience that*. And what it is remembering is that the best way to have this experience is by *not doing anything*. There is nothing to do but to be.[7]

If we define ourselves by our relationships, that is better than identifying solely with a job, for experiencing relationships is one of the primary reasons for choosing to enter into human life. But then we need to flesh out the picture by listing all our relationships– wife/husband, mother/father, daughter/son, sister/brother, niece/nephew, cousin, friend, etc. Identifying ourselves in terms of significant relationships is closer to *beingness* than limiting our self-view to what we do for work or play, but it still does not tell us who we are inside. Listing the types of relationships we have chosen tells us only to whom we relate, not who we are.

If someone had asked you at earlier times in your life who you are, what would you have said? You could not have identified yourself by job type or other role in adult life. Nor could you have listed as many types of relationships as you now have. Most likely you would have responded with a combination of the two. "I am a student at Big City High School" and "Phil and Alice Smith's son." Before you were old enough to see yourself as a student, you might have simply replied with your name. "I am John Paul Smith." If pressed at age three or four to add what else you are, you might possibly pipe up with, "I'm a boy."

Do you remember your need to fit in during your school years? You may have believed that the right clothes, shoes, and "toys" would impress your classmates. Peer pressure was extremely important to you then. You did not want to be different; you wanted to be "cool." Your main desire was to be accepted as part of the group, not to stand out from it.

You have altered how you see yourself over the years because what is important to you has changed.

Do you see how your views of yourself have changed over the course of time? Does that mean *you* are someone different now? Or does it mean you have changed your perspective? Changed the things with which you identify. You might at this point say, "Well, of course I've changed. I *am* different now." That is a valid point. Yet, though your body has grown, and changed along the way, is it the same body or a different one? And, while the activities in which you engage now are vastly different than when you were three, or thirteen, does that mean the person you are inside is a different person? No, you are the same soul, but your thinking has evolved.

You have been accustomed to thinking of yourself in so many ways. And you have changed your beliefs about who you are, and about what is important in the world, so many times. Can you handle one more evolution in thought? Can you accept that you are, in fact, a Light Being and not a human being?

Question 5: If you are a soul and not a human being, and you existed before the body you inhabit was born, how did you get into the body?

Discussion: The "knowings" I received on this subject while merged with Source explained that human religious doctrines about souls entering into human form simply do not go far enough. Religion glosses over the part about the soul existing as a separate being from the body. Rather, souls are characterized in the Bible as coming directly from God without elaboration. If that is true, how does the soul get into the human fetus? Does it enter in the form of breath like the Book of Genesis claims?

"Knowings" informed me that souls do come from Source, indirectly, through the extensions of Source's self-awareness that humans would perceive as Beings of Light.

Think of Source's Energy radiating outwardly through the universe like Light, similar to how our sun's rays radiate toward the planets in our solar system. With human eyes, we perceive Source's Energy as physical matter: planets, stars, galaxies, and the universe at large. After our humans' deaths, we go into "the Light." This phrase can be taken literally. Once we leave human bodies, and their visual restrictions, we actually see Source's Energy as Light. Source's radiating love is not only felt but also visually perceived as Light.

After creating our physical universe, Source disbursed its own self-awareness, consciousness, and identity outward into facets or fragments of itself. This was much like how Source radiates its Energy as Light. We are those facets of Source. We are actually part and parcel of the entity we call God. What we perceive to be our own separate lives are in reality merely thoughts, creations, imaginings, whatever we wish to call it, transpiring in the mind of Source. We are manifestations of Source's desire to know experientially, rather than intellectually, what it would be like to be each one of US.

Each of Source's facets or fragments is just concentrated Energy, but it appears to human eyes as a "being." That is, the human brain interprets the Energy pattern of one of Source's facets or fragments to be the outline of a glowing humanoid body. This is why near-death experiencers see humanoid spiritual beings while they are dead. The Energy patterns existing at the vibrational level we call heaven, or the Light, are what other near-death experiencers and I call Light Beings.

We are those Light Beings, not human beings. As Beings of Light, we are integral parts of Source's self-awareness, consciousness, and identity. We are ultimately undivided facets or fragments of Source's thoughts, though from lower vibrational levels we appear to be separate Beings of Light. Because we are facets of Source, we have the same innate ability that Source does to outwardly extend part of our own self-awareness, consciousness, and identity to become the soul of a human animal.

Unlike humans, Light Beings enjoy multiple simultaneous layers of awareness (discussed in Chapter 20 of *BACKWARDS: Returning to Our Source for Answers*). Picture one of those consciousness layers being separated out and its vibration lowered. That lowered Energy becomes what we call a "soul." It enters into a chosen human animal before its birth. From the perspective of the Light Being Energy remaining in the Light, the part of its Energy that became a soul seems to be unconscious or asleep because its level of self-awareness has been so greatly diminished. From the perspective of the Light Being Energy that entered into the human, it lives a lifetime believing itself to be human.

Human Perspective	Light Being Perspective	Source's Perspective
I exist as a human being with an immortal soul.	I infuse some of my Energy into a human to serve as its soul. That Energy will experience life as a human, while the rest of my Energy remains in spiritual form in the Light.	I have partitioned my own personality into many segments, each of which believes it is a separate Light Being until it merges back into me.

One benefit of understanding the three levels of perspective is that it gives us the choice of raising our sites to a higher level. We have the ability to enrich our enlightenment by shifting our beliefs to a higher perspective before we actually achieve it.

The greater importance of understanding, and believing, the three levels of perspective outlined above is the power it gives us. If we accept that only part of our Energy is in the body we inhabit, and that another part remains in the Light of Source's love and Energy, then we have a built-in conduit for accessing all of our Light Being powers. We can from time-to-time achieve total recall of our eternal lives, Universal Knowledge, conscious manifesting, multiple simultaneous levels of awareness, and unconditional love. We can literally pray to ourselves for answers. We can emotionally support ourselves with love beyond anything humans have to offer. We can heal ourselves. We can take conscious control of our manifesting in order to improve our human lives. We can reach far beyond the physical limitations of the bodies we inhabit to achieve greater peace and happiness.

Knowing who we really are opens us up to our true power, as shown by the following chart:

Human Perspective	Light Being Perspective	Source's Perspective
I am limited to human abilities.	As part of Source, I have all of Source's abilities at a lower power level.	I am all-powerful.

We are incredibly exciting, fascinating, multi-dimensional beings—Beings of Light and Love—with a wide range of levels of awareness and self-awareness. Added on top is a delicious sauce of humanity. We have chosen to experience the life of a human animal and see as it sees. Sense as it senses. Feel as it feels. For a while. After we have accomplished what we have chosen for this human adventure, we will depart physical life and resume living the spiritual life we have enjoyed for eons.

Still not convinced? We can *choose* to become aware of and get to know our real self. The simple truth of two beings within one body can be easily proven. We can do it just by exercising our powers of observation as discussed in Chapter 5.

4

✳ What Is the Purpose of Life?

ALL MY RELIGIOUS AND spiritual studies before my death had lulled me into believing I understood the purpose of life, which in my mind had nothing to do with how I spent my time. So foolish. I was so blinded by the American dream that Source had to literally kill me before I got the message: the key to a fulfilling life begins with having a clearer sense of who we really are—*cherished, powerful, literal extensions of our Creator.*

Speculation abounds on the purpose of human life. The consensus among philosophers and religious leaders seems to be that we are here to learn.

But *what* are we to learn?

Many say we are here to learn love. Yes, we seek to remember how to love unconditionally though embroiled in animal instincts of survival, violence, and territoriality. Trying to live as a loving being while in a human animal body is very difficult. Humans are animals, with animal drives, instincts, and morality. Just as a lion feels no guilt when devouring its prey, the human animal, unguided by the soul within, may feel no guilt about killing others he deems to be a competitor or threat of some kind (even merely a threat to the ego). Our laws allowing murder in self-defense is an acknowledgement of this animal trait. So too are our governments' positions on war. Killing in war—even mass murder—is permitted because humans are fighting to defend their territory, or to preserve natural resources needed for survival. These are purely animal perspectives with resulting animal morality.

A soul that chooses the life of a mass murderer may have done so for the challenge it presents: the struggle to control animal drives. The soul may not be strong enough while trapped in the body to be able to prevent its murderous rampage. Or, the soul may be new to human incarnation or completely unaware of its own true nature. In all these instances the combined being's actions are more often dictated by animal nature than Light Being nature.

It may take many, many lifetimes in a human body for the soul inside to learn how to control the host's animal instincts, and much longer to be able to express love. That is why enlightenment is so incredibly important. We have to be aware of who we really are in order to even know that we have the option of controlling our host bodies' behavior. And Earth conditions will not improve so long as we continue to allow our bodies to make decisions based on animal instincts.

Part of our mission on Earth is to demonstrate unconditional

43

love while in human form, even in the most difficult of circumstances. But our ultimate purpose is far greater. To understand this more fully we must go back to creation.

Source created the universe in order to appreciate the physical and emotional sensations associated with its all-knowingness. Source knew intellectually everything that it could ever imagine. But it had no sensations equivalent to what we call "experience."

While in human bodies we are keenly aware of the difference between knowing about an event and actually living through it. We can watch the movie *Titanic* and dream of saving the beautiful young lady. But we are well aware that neither watching the movie nor imagining ourselves as the hero comes anywhere close to actually surviving a shipwreck. We have to *feel* the terror of watching the decks tilt, the splash of cold sea water swirling up our legs, and the desperation of fighting our way to a lifeboat, to be able to say we have "experienced" shipwreck.

Source *experiences* what it already knows about physical life by manifesting us to live it.

Manifesting means literally creating physical reality as we know it by the force of one's "attention and intention." Source focused its attention upon creating a physical universe with the intention that it expand, live, and eventually evolve back to Source. Scientists' "big bang" theory is not too far off from how the universe was actually created. That theory merely avoids identifying the original Source of all the Energy that went "bang."

We can use the model of dreaming as an analogy for how Source manifested our universe. Manifesting is not dreaming, of course, for manifesting truly creates reality. Dreaming does not. But dreaming is an activity we all understand that can provide us with a framework for understanding creation.

"Knowings" about dreams downloaded directly into my mind shortly after I entered the Light. What I remember is that humans have three types of experiences we call dreams: a filing and storage function, a type of body/soul communication, and consciously manifested living.

Filing and storage dreams are little visions or stories our brains make up as it processes the day's events and files useful information away for later retrieval. Some scientists believe this is the only type of dream we have—that all dreams are brain functions. Filing and storage dreams examine our recent actions, emotions, and thoughts, and all external data we absorbed, and sort items for proper categorization and integration. For example, we may learn something during the day that helps us understand why children act as they do. We then file it in our child-rearing memories through dreaming. Or a neighbor may pass us on the sidewalk, trailing Old Spice aftershave in his wake. We unconsciously associate that scent with our neighbor through filing and storage dreams. Generally, if we recognize something from our day in a dream, like a character from TV or the playground at the local elementary school, it is most likely a filing and storage dream.

Dreams

2   The second category of dream serves a body/soul communication function. These dreams are designed to focus the sleeping human's attention on a physical or emotional condition of which the sleeper is unaware. The classic example is dreaming that our arm is injured, when in reality it is "asleep" because our sleeping position has limited blood flow. The resident soul knows the arm is in danger and that the sleeping human is not aware of it. So it manufactures a dream that startles the body into waking and repositioning. Nightmares serve this purpose well.

3   Another example is a communication dream I used to have when I was doing a lot of flying. I would dream that I was happily piloting my flying club airplane over acres of cornfields or busy city streets. Then the plane would stall and nose-dive. But instead of crashing and killing me, the little Cessna would either level out at the last minute or simply dissolve, leaving me standing unharmed on the ground. After a number of these dreams, I realized I was trying to make my conscious mind aware of the fact that a relationship important to me was about to crash from neglect of brewing problems. I used flying as a metaphor for relationships.

Communication dreams are the ones psychologists say use symbolism rather than direct messaging. We have to interpret them to understand their meaning.

The last category of dreams is not dreaming at all. Some of what we call dreaming is actually manifesting. As purely spiritual beings, we do not require sleep. So while our hosts sleep, we continue living without them. Some of what we remember as dreams is actually manifested reality we have lived through without the body. We can usually tell manifested reality from dreaming by the degree to which we are convinced it was "real." For example, I shop a lot in my nighttime life—probably because my body hates it. Often, when I buy clothes during this manifested reality, I am so convinced I actually bought them that I will expect to see them in my closet the next day.

Perhaps you have heard yourself say, "I could have sworn I didn't dream that." Perhaps you are right. You may have lived the events through manifesting while your body slept.

Nightly manifested living can place us in a different life, a different body, or even on a different planet. We can manufacture environments we have only imagined and enjoy them as completely real. We can play superhero with physical abilities unavailable to mortal men. Flying (without an airplane) dreams may be manifested living, rather than merely symbolic.

Another feature of manifested living is the accessibility of past, present, and future. There is no "time" without a body that senses time. So it is possible to "dream" the future and have it come true. We can meet people, visit places, and do things in dreams and then repeat those events in waking life. Our dreams then seem to be prophetic of future events, or omens.

Source's creation of the universe is like the third category of dream, in which we actually manifest and experience physical reality. Source manifested us to engage in the physical activities it knows intellectually, so that it can experience them first hand. It is our *privilege* to serve our Creator this way. We live so that our Source may more fully explore its own intelligence and creativity.

That is our ultimate purpose.

Human Perspective	Light Being Perspective	Source's Perspective
God created me as a human being to learn how to love and serve him.	My purpose is to experience the physical universe Source created by extending my own self-awareness into physical matter.	I am gaining experiential knowledge of all I know intellectually through thought-forms designed to believe they are individuals apart from me.

But, are we also here to *learn?*

Yes, and no. Because our ultimate purpose is to experience all that Source and we can imagine, we collectively live through all three hundred and sixty degrees of every possible aspect of human life. We witness it intimately from all angles and perspectives, and within all combinations of relationships. Doing so will seem like we are supposed to be learning something specifically about ourselves. And perhaps we are, but it is only so that we may exhaust one viewpoint and move on to the next.

We are *not* here to learn how to be good enough to enter

"I AM NOT A SOUL, I AM NOT A SOUL!"

heaven. Everyone reaches the state we call heaven upon his/her body's death.

Nor has Source tasked us with achieving perfection while in human form. We evolve to higher and higher spiritual levels because that is our nature. It is automatic. The mechanics are built right into us. We cannot escape evolution back to our Source. All we can do is increase or decrease the speed by our choice of behavior. Developing greater awareness increases evolution. Sticking our heads in the sand by denying our true spiritual nature slows it down.

In the grand scheme of things, we do learn by virtue of experience, time, and repetition what human life feels like, while at the same time our animal bodies are being trained how to survive. We also have the opportunity each lifetime to work through, and resolve, the many erroneous beliefs and emotional traumas imbedded in our eternal personalities via human life. And we evolve with each new experience. But not everything about human life holds a spiritual lesson.

What are we to learn about ourselves from others' broken promises, lost loves, floods and famines, defective appliances, serial killers, or someone stealing our parking spot at the grocery store? Surely not every event in our lives is a teaching tool, for so many of them appear to be outside our control. How are we to prevent the damage from tornadoes? What can we do as private citizens to eliminate crime? What have we done to deserve being treated rudely or being sold defective goods?

*　　*　　*

Question 1: What do you believe we are supposed to learn from pain, suffering, and the evil and hardship in the world?

Discussion: Many believe that our higher power can, but chooses not to, protect us from harm. We think Source sees us suffering and does nothing about it because we are supposed to "learn" from our pain. To learn humility and trust in the Lord. But what kind of person trusts someone who abuses him/her? Only a beaten down, hope-deprived creature that has become accustomed to abuse trusts its tormentor. Is that how we really see ourselves? As beaten down, hopeless creatures at the mercy of a tormenting deity? And what exactly are we supposed to learn from pain allegedly inflicted by Source?

My belief before my beyond death experience was that pain and suffering are inherent in human life by design. I had been told, "God does not give us more than we can handle."

But often my burdens *felt* like more than I could handle. So I tried to glean some good from misfortune by learning a lesson from each of the troubles that befell me. Usually those lessons had something to do with what was *wrong* with *me*—what I had done to deserve such bad luck. Or I was trying to figure out how to avoid repeating that calamity. I wanted to know how to *control* my life to avoid pain. Now, of course, I know I was mistaken about all that. I had it backwards.

Source did not intend pain and suffering to be inherent in human life, beyond that occasioned by physical illness or injury. Source intends for us to enjoy physical life and all the adventures it brings.

Source thought us into existence composed of its own Energy. We are thus invested with all the same innate character traits. One of Source's most endearing qualities passed on to us is its joyous nature. We can use that innate spiritual nature here on Earth to create more joyful lives. We have the ability to live joyfully regardless of our circumstances because joy is built right into our very nature as extensions of Source.

Human judgmental nature is what steals our joy. We cannot let go of the idea that bad behavior must be punished. So we have constructed belief systems around that core falsehood. Always there must be a lesson to be learned, according to our beliefs. A correction made in our lives. We must move toward perfection in our thoughts and deeds in order to be "saved." For every bad deed we must make amends through suffering or performing counterbalancing good deeds. Or so we think.

Yet who decides what is "good" and what is "bad?" Humans do! Not Source. Nothing we can think, say, or do is considered "bad" by Source because it arises *from* the creative mind of Source. All we are, all we do, all we think and feel and say is an act of

Source because we *are* Source. We are literal extensions of Source's innate nature and self-awareness. And Source does not condemn its own behavior. Nor does it judge it. It simply is not in Source's nature to be judgmental.

Source does not punish. I learned that during my life review with my five Light Being friends.

I was also shown that there was nothing wrong with me that brought on all the disasters in my human life. All was as it should have been—for an unawakened soul *unconsciously* manifesting its destiny. And I was not the only one. There are millions and millions of unawakened souls out there manifesting reality completely oblivious to their own motivations. Most have no idea they are even capable of creating physical reality. They believe reality exists out there somewhere, independent of us. So it is no surprise that all these manifestations at cross-purposes cause conflict and even harm.

We were created to experience all we individually and collectively can imagine. Some of these events will be painful because in human form we can, and do, imagine and act out some very hurtful and destructive scenarios. These outcomes are the natural consequence of the interplay between innate human violence and our own free will choices. They are not lessons constructed by Source to teach us what is wrong with us.

There was, however, a lesson I could have learned—the one I finally did learn by dying: I was unconsciously manifesting unhappy experiences, alone and in concert with others, because I did not know any better. I was unaware of the fact that I have the innate power to *consciously* manifest happier and healthier experiences. I cannot change all the events of my life, especially those involving other people. We co-create with others and cannot deny their freedom of choice. But I can change how I *experience* my life. I can make better choices for myself.

All I needed to change the tide of my life was to realize I had been unconsciously acting out lifetimes of learned behavior and emotional baggage. (More on this in Chapter 9.)

Human Perspective	Light Being Perspective	Source's Perspective
I am here to learn how to get into Heaven.	I am here to experience all aspects of humanity and then I will return to Source.	My creations are experiencing physical life for me. They will merge back into me, giving me intimate access to all their experiences.

* * *

Question 2: If we are not here to learn from the pain and evil in the world, then why does Source allow horrific events to occur?

Discussion: Think of it this way. Every night we go to sleep and dream, sometimes of things we would not do during waking life. Take the example of a nightmare. Have you ever dreamed that you were on an airplane when it crashed killing everyone on board? Or that you were arguing with someone and pushed him down in anger, only to discover that he died on impact with a sharp object on the ground? Or maybe you dreamed you were in a traffic accident and survived, but you severely injured the other driver? Do nightmares like this seem very real to you at the time?

"Yes, they do," you say.

Do you sometimes wake up from a nightmare screaming, crying, or sweating because you felt genuine fright?

"Yes."

The next morning do you turn yourself in to the police, saying "I killed a hundred and fifty-seven people on an airplane last night?" Or do you confess to pushing someone down and killing him? Or to reckless endangerment for your driving that caused injuries to the other driver in your accident?

"Of course not," you say, "that's ridiculous."

Why is it ridiculous?

"Because it didn't really happen. It was just a dream."

That is right. It was just a dream. But those things did really happen while you were dreaming them, and, they felt very real to your dream characters, including you. It was not until you woke up from sleep that you began to believe those nightmarish events were not real.

From our earliest awareness of human life, we have been accustomed to sleeping and dreaming. We know in our bones, and from our parents, that dreaming is a natural process of living. Everyone does it. It is a biological fact. The normalcy of dreaming goes a long way toward relieving any anxiety we might feel about the consequences to dream characters when we wake. We are carried the rest of the way by our belief that dream characters are not "real." They are figments of our imagination—even the ones who also exist in waking life, like friends and family. "It's almost as if our waking selves and sleeping selves are two separate beings living in alternate dimensions, never catching more than a passing glimpse of each other."[8]

Only physical matter is real, or so we tell ourselves. Non-physical dream characters cannot be. If they were never real in the first place, their deaths upon waking likewise are not real. We feel comfortable waking up guiltless. This is the human level of perspective. Remember that guiltless feeling when reading the following about higher levels of perspective.

I was quite shocked to discover, during my beyond death experience, that when we are in our natural spirit form, we do not consider human life to be real at all. In comparison to the more intense, expansive sense of reality we feel in the afterlife, the human adventure the soul Energy undertakes no longer has the feel of reality. We view the *experiences* we garner while encased in a human body to be real, but human life itself takes on the air of unreality, as though it were virtual reality, or a play, or drug-induced mind trip. We know for a fact that we, in concert with other Light Beings, have used our spiritual powers to manifest the Earthly environment—in much the same way we individually manifest human dream environments.

While we are living human life it seems very, very real. We suffer intense pain over physical and emotional injuries. We truly grieve the loss of a loved one. We feel the pitfalls and thrills of daily life. It is real to us. But, much as dreams are only reality while we sleep, human life is only reality while we are experiencing it.

Similarly, once we have awakened to our full Light Being level of awareness, we no longer value human life as dearly as we did while living it. Our sense of reality has shifted so much that abandoning our former human bodies seems no more Earth-shattering than waking up from sleep. We suffer no guilt that a human animal had to die for us to awaken into the afterlife. We realize that we can manifest our physical identity again any time we want it. So its loss feels less acute. Once having come to terms with the realization that physical life is but our own manifestation, our own thoughts, we do not mourn the tragedies we know humans endure any more than we grieved the horrors our dream characters suffered during human nightmares. They are not real. What happens on Earth is of no more consequence than what happens in human dreams.

Ultimately, when the Light Being fuses back into Source, the

Light Being will realize that even its perceived separate existence is not reality. Once again a shift in vantage point produces new understanding. The Light Being will finally know its true nature as an undivided part of Source. It will know that it never actually separated from Source, despite very convincing evidence to the contrary. This revelation does not make the Light Being's life in the Light any less real at the time it was occurring. But, once having achieved Source's own perspective on creation, the Light Being will accept that its lower levels of perspective were just that—perception, not reality.

That is how Source can allow horrible things to happen to humans. The events are not real. They are manifestations without eternal consequences. Source can allow bad things to happen on Earth the same way we can allow ourselves in dreams to crash an airplane and kill all passengers and crew aboard, or push someone to his death, or have an automobile accident that maims and mangles innocent strangers. To Source, human life is mere creative imagery in its own mind—just as dreams exist only in our minds. No "real" harm is done, no matter how it feels to us now.

Each perspective—Source's, Light Being's, and human's—is valid. Each is real. Each level of consciousness experiences the reality Source intended for it. Each level of Source's Energy views life from a different perspective, resulting in what might appear to be conflicting truths.

Human Perspective	Light Being Perspective	Source's Perspective
Human life is real.	Human life is a "dream" one part of me is having, or a role part of my Energy is playing. Human life is not real.	Energy Beings are parts of me playing roles via different personalities so that I may experience physical life through separate existences. None of it is real.

＊　＊　＊

Question 3: Do you believe negative energy and evil truly exist in the world, and that they are responsible for some of the horrible things that happen?

Discussion: All Energy comes from Source. There is no such thing as negative Energy. How could Energy coming from an unconditionally loving being be negative?

There is no evil entity. No Devil. No evil spirits. No monsters under the bed—except, of course, for human monsters.

All creations are part of Source, which is the ultimate loving entity in our universe.

Do we really believe that Source created monsters to devour us? A Devil to lead us astray? Evil spirits to roam the Earth and pose a threat to us? We can only believe such things if we refuse to believe that Source is all loving. We can only accept such beliefs if we allow human fear to determine our reality.

Source created us specifically to have physical experiences. All types of physical experiences. There are no limits set. No boundaries we may not cross. Our free will is unrestricted. Our creativity is allowed full roam. We may choose to have any experience at all, including those humans judge to be evil. This is because Source does not have it in its nature to judge us! All experiences—disabilities, criminal behavior, suicide—all manner of physical sensations are what Source seeks through us.

We choose to inhabit human hosts because of the wealth of physical and emotional traits they offer that are foreign to our spiritual nature: fear, violence, lust, greed, competition, and bodily sensations. We are not here to "rise above" being human. We are here *to be* human. We are not expected to overcome innate human characteristics, like sexuality and fear, in order to become worthy of entering heaven.

I saw with my own eyes that we reincarnate over and over in order to experience every conceivable type of event, emotion, sensation, thought, word, and deed of which a human is capable. Our lifetime choices include ones humans would label "bad" or "evil" because that is necessary to round out a three hundred and sixty degree perspective on humanity.

The only evil in this world arises from humans. Our human hosts engage in unspeakable acts because they are animals. We, the souls within, choose to act badly out of curiosity, ignorance, or learned human behavior.

No outside force is responsible for evil or catastrophe. It is an inside job. Innate survival instinct in the case of human behavior. Unenlightened free will in the case of soul behavior.

Question 4: Do you believe there *must be* punishment, or at least some form of accountability in the afterlife for our actions? Why else would anyone be motivated to be good? If the bad go to heaven the same as the good, what's the point in trying to be good?

Discussion: Many believe that even if we escape punishment for something "bad" we have done in this lifetime, we will suffer the consequences either in our next incarnation (for those who believe in reincarnation) or in the afterlife. There must be consequences, we say to ourselves, lest human behavior run amok. Therein lies the truth about our belief in punishment. It disguises our belief in the need for control. Control through threatening punishment. Control through meting out punishment. Humans must be controlled because of their innate violence. That may be true. But.

We project this belief in control onto the afterlife because we assume we will continue to be human there. We will not be human beings living in a spiritual heaven. We are not human beings now. We are spiritual beings inhabiting human hosts. And we will return to spiritual form after departing these beings of flesh. We will exist as Beings of Light living spiritual lives very different from what we are used to now. We will not carry human nature into the afterlife. Fear, violence, control, and punishment will disappear with the human personalities we leave in the grave. They are not part of who we really are. They are not traits of the Source.

Reincarnation does not exist in order for us to make amends for one life with another. Human life is a privilege—not punishment. We take human form over and over in order to round out our perspectives. One lifetime on Earth gives us a very stilted and one-dimensional view of what being human means.

Source does not judge or punish us for what we did in human life. Near-death experiencers (NDErs) who have had a life review almost unanimously report that *they* were the only one judging their human life. Not Source.

More importantly, NDErs report the same phenomenon that I encountered while my life review played out—we could *feel* every single thing we had caused another to feel. One NDE survivor has described it so beautifully and accurately this way:

FLASH! Brilliant colors came radiating from within me, to be displayed in front of us [she was with a group of persons whose faces radiated unconditional love], like a theater floating in air. It was a three-dimensional, panoramic view of my life, every aspect of my life. Everything I had ever said or done, or even thought, was right there, for all of us to experience. I rethought every thought, I reexperienced every feeling, as it happened, in an instant. When I had passed judgment on someone else, I would experience myself doing that. Then I would change places in perspective, and experience what that judgment had felt like for them to receive from me. Then I'd return to my own feelings, to be able to respond to the drama I'd just witnessed and experienced, to react, for example, with shame or remorse because of that episode. Multitudinous actions or thoughts, derived from my own meanness, unkindness, or anger, caused me to feel the consequent pains of the other people. I experienced this even if at the time I had hurt someone, I had chosen to ignore how that would affect them. And I felt their pain for the full length of time they were affected by what I had done. Because I was in a different dimension where time can't be measured, as we know time to exist on earth, it was possible to know all of this and experience it all at once, in a moment, and with the ability to comprehend all of this information![9]

What could be more just than for us to suffer the same pains we once inflicted on others? And to do so voluntarily, spontaneously, as we review our human behaviors in the afterlife with the perspective of unconditional love inherent in our spiritual nature? WE will be the judge and jury. We will sentence ourselves to the same emotions our actions elicited in others. Does it not seem fair that during his life review Hitler suffered all the torture his concentration camp inmates endured because of him? And that once Hitler saw what he had done through the lens of unconditional love, that he was mortified, remorseful, and full of self-loathing? Can you think of a more fitting punishment than to endure precisely what we caused another to feel for as long as they felt it?

* * *

Question 5: Do you believe we are supposed to stay on a life path that destiny and/or the deity created for us? How are we to do that if there are no guideposts along the way in the form of lessons or taboos?

Discussion: Human life is a lot like walking my friend Lucy the dog down the bike path in my neighborhood. She stays mostly on the path, but veers off, and sometimes stops, when an interesting smell arrests her senses. But even with all the stops, and starts, and detours, Lucy eventually gets the job done.

So do we.

We are here just to live—to meander down life's primrose path to see where it leads.

If we are here to experience a particular aspect of humanity, it will be built right into the life circumstances of the human we have chosen to inhabit. That is why we chose him or her. If we have a special task to perform, we will unconsciously put ourselves in a position to perform it. And, if all else fails, a sudden spiritual awakening will open our eyes just at the precise moment we need it to jumpstart us on the assigned project.

We cannot fail at life. So there is no need for route markers or boundaries.

✳   ✳   ✳

Question 6: Do you believe that everything happens for a

reason, that there are no coincidences? And that if you could just *see* that reason you could make the right decisions?

Discussion: Everything does happen for a reason. Everything that happens has been manifested by one or more of us as agents of Source. But that does not mean that everything we encounter holds an express message for our own personal direction in life. What happens here fulfills the overall purpose of collecting physical experiences for Source. Each moment holds the golden opportunity for experiencing and knowing human life. But not every moment waives a sign telling us what to do or where to go.

We co-create human life with all others who have chosen it. Much of what we do is by agreement with other Light Beings. Certain events may be for another's benefit rather than our own. For example, a dear friend of mine is struggling to understand why she was in an auto accident. She wants desperately to know what lesson she is to learn. I have tried telling her, "stuff happens." But that answer is not satisfying. The complete answer may well be that there was never any intention that *she* learn something from this tragedy. She may have just been along for the ride, so to speak, in order for someone else to experience what it is like to be in an accident.

Try to let go of the notion that our lives are planned and that everything has deep significance. The more we use human analytical skills to try to discern meaning in our lives, the less we are able to listen for the very information we desire to come to us from Universal Knowledge. Remember, only part of our Light Being Energy is in the human bodies we inhabit. The rest is still in the Light guiding us to meet our intended goals. Just sit back and allow that to happen naturally. Enjoy life, and it will unfold for you just as you intended when you decided to come here.

＊　　＊　　＊

Question 7: Our purpose is to have physical experiences for Source. But why would Source want to experience a life of abuse or drug-addiction, or to die a violent death?

Discussion: Source desires to experience all that it can imagine, pleasurable as well as painful. Source and Light Beings do not make judgments that one life is better or more rewarding than another. All lives provide experiences. And that is the goal.

Although a lifetime of abuse can drag like a million years while experiencing it in the body, once we are out-of-body and restored to our spiritual state it represents only one second of our eternal lives. There is no time outside the body. The only time is the present—the one second of the eternal "now." So to a Light Being, one second of pain, drug-dependence, or violence seems worth it to find out what that type of life feels like. It is much like the child who touches the stove after being told it is hot—he wants to experience what "hot" means. Our natural curiosity as Light Beings can overcome any trepidation we may feel about enduring pain and suffering in a human life.

Most importantly, we Light Beings are capable of *unconditionally loving* the abuser spouses, the alcoholics, the drug addicts, and the violent types among mankind. Unconditional love means no value judgment is made of a human life. No blame cast. No guilt felt. No condemnation of behavior. Each and every life is loved completely, without reservation, fear, or preference. We Light Beings do not reject a human life just because it presents problems.

Human Perspective	Light Being Perspective	Source's Perspective
God will punish me for my sins here or in the afterlife.	I am the only one who will judge my life during my life review.	I do not judge.

Part II – Applying the Lessons Learned

Part II of *BACKWARDS: Returning to Our Source for Answers* builds on the Universal Knowledge principles of Part I by showing how they can be applied in our daily lives. The Chapters entitled: Living a New Way of Thinking, Wake UP! Who's in Charge? What Is And Isn't Unconditional Love, Reeducation, Self-Healing, Stop Judging, Treat Each Other Responsibly, Manifest Consciously, and Light Up Religious Institutions, outline a plan for living using the innate powers we all have as Beings of Light.

The chapters in Part II of this *Guidebook* coordinate with those in Part II of the first book and continue the discussion in more detail. Examples from everyday life are given to illustrate the various spiritual concepts.

5

Wake UP!

MANY OF US HAVE a concept of "enlightenment," becoming aware of insights and truths more spiritual than our everyday thoughts. But, aside from the unexpected awakening, oftentimes we do not know how to reach enlightenment. We cannot raise our awareness level at will, or on a time schedule consistent with our hectic lives. Is there a secret formula to producing insight? A foolproof plan for gaining spiritual knowledge?

Yes. *We* must wake up! We have to learn the difference between our host bodies being awake and being awake *ourselves*. "Waking up is being mindful of living in the moment while living in truth and with gratitude. It also means that your actions are conducted with the intention of serving your highest good and the highest good of those around you."[10] You must first be awake before you can be enlightened.

The secret to predictable enlightenment is learning how to

access Universal Knowledge through our Energy Being level of existence—through that part of us that remains in the Light and connected to the knowledge of the universe. Gaining "knowings" is effortless and instant when living in the Light, but not such a snap while in the body.

The key to accessing Universal Knowledge is to use "attention and intention." Give your undivided attention by concentrating on the question at hand. Then form the intention to have the answer. Ask, and then listen. Ask yourself, or the universe, or God, if you prefer, the question on your mind with the firm expectation that it will be answered. Then wait and listen for insight.

It is the listening that most often eludes us. We all constantly think. We hear words in our minds that form the background music of our existence—a monologue on our daily lives, as well as a death sentence to our ability to listen. We must silence that mental voice, that stream of consciousness as we call it.

There are a number of ways to silence our minds. Many are described in Eckhart Tolle's book *The Power of Now*.[11] Others include meditation, Reiki, massage, sitting in a hot tub, weight lifting, Chi Gong, Tai Chi, running, and anything else that will allow us to step back mentally and emotionally and see our bodies objectively. Al-Anon has the perfect phrase for it: "detach with love." Detach with love from your body so that you can observe its thoughts and emotions without being part of them. Then consciously shut off mental input from the body.

*　　*　　*

Exercise 1: Just stop the flow of words running through your mind. Shut them out. Make your mind a blank. Concentrate on being silent. Breathe. Feel the air around you. Hear the sounds of your environment. But do not attach any words to those sensations. Do not think, "I can feel myself breathing." Do not say to yourself, "It's hot in here." Do not let the words, "That sounds like Fido barking," enter your mind. Be wordless for as long as you can.

Discussion: No matter how good you are at keeping your mind blank, eventually some words will creep in. A thought will form. It might be, "My nose itches." Or, "This is stupid." It does not matter what the words are. What matters is that you can see them, hear them, entering your mind. You are standing back and observing your own mind at work. How could you do that if there is only one being in there?

> When you are aware that you are thinking, that awareness is not part of thinking. It is a different dimension of consciousness. And it is that awareness that says "I am." If there were nothing but thought in you, you wouldn't even know you are thinking. You would be like a dreamer who doesn't know he is dreaming. You would be as identified with every thought as the dreamer is with every image in the dream.[12]

In this passage from the book *A New Earth*, Eckhart Tolle explains how we can know that there are two identities in one body. One is doing the thinking. The other is standing back and observing the thinking behavior. Two consciousnesses. Two aware beings. Two. And we are the ones watching our human hosts think.

Now that you have shifted from thinker to observer role, you have exercised one form of your innate Light Being ability to hold multiple simultaneous levels of awareness. You have experienced the consciousness of two different beings. You have briefly experienced life as one who can objectively witness thoughts—the witnessing presence. And you have experienced life as the thinker who has been unaware all these years that another level of consciousness inhabits its body.

In our natural Light Being state, free of a physical body, we move effortlessly between and among many more levels of perspective and awareness. If this sounds like an impossible task, remember that you may have done the same thing with the aid of sleep or drugs. Here are examples:

❋   ❋   ❋

Example A: You are dreaming in the morning close to wake-up time, a lovely dream of a party where you are the guest of honor. You are having a wonderful time and want to party forever. Unwillingly, you become aware of a small glint of light through your eyelids. You hear the furnace kick on to warm your home before you have to get out of bed. The smell of coffee brewing wafts through the cool air, tickling your taste buds. These clues let you know it is almost time to get up.

But you do not want to leave the party. You are just about to make a speech about how honored you feel by your friends, family, and business colleagues. The words you have prepared are on the tip of your tongue. A flute of champagne fizzes in your hand, its bubbles not nearly as light and sparkling as you feel. You rehearse your lines a couple of times in anticipation of the ending of the too flattering toast in your honor. You desperately want to hear the full introduction, all the kind words, the tributes, and the list of your accomplishments.

The daylight in your bedroom grows, burning red behind your eyelids. Your stomach flips in anticipation of waffles and coffee. You fight to keep your focus on the party. Yet the bubble bursts and you can no longer remember your lines. The party scene evaporates and you open your eyes.

Who was attending the party? You? Part of you? Which part? Who was waking up to the aroma of Columbian coffee beans? How many of you are there?

Discussion: Some stages of analysis in this example are obvious, you may say. Clearly while the dream party was developing, and before light, heat, and coffee smells intruded, "you" were asleep. Your body was not actually attending a party. That event transpired entirely in your mind. How can your mind go to a party and leave your body behind in slumber? "Easy," you say, "that is the normal process of dreaming." What then is dreaming? Is it a function of the body? Mind? Both?

You might be correct in saying that "you" are awake once the light, coffee, and furnace grab your attention so much that you can no longer reconstruct the dream and return to it.

What then of the in-between stage? The stage where you are first distracted by the light trying to pry open your eyelids? The point where you can still elect to return to the party, take your bows, and revel in the glory of being the center of attention? Are you awake or asleep? Is your mind awake and dreaming while your body catches forty winks? Or maybe it is only twenty winks since the body is starting to awaken. Which role are "you" playing? The dreamer or the sleeper? Your answer may well be that "you" are both. You are vacillating between dreaming and waking. Do you mean your body, or your mind, is swerving in and out of the dream state? If you are dreaming, according to scientists your body is paralyzed[13] and is not awake. And it seems like your mind is totally awake because it is whooping it up at a party. Are "you" split in two?

Could it be that instead of "you" actually going back and forth between honored guest and sleepyhead, it is your attention or awareness shifting from one to the other state? Could it be that so long as you maintain your attention to the dream, and the body stays asleep, you can still capture the toastmaster's kudos? And, is the body awakening against "your" will? The body is waking up in response to physical stimuli because that is its nature—its physical nature.

If the body responds to physical changes, like smells and sunlight, against "your" will, whose will is it to awaken? Who's in charge? And who else is in there to be in charge of?

Do you agree now that we are capable of multiple levels of awareness, and not just the ones we call awake and asleep?

✳   ✳   ✳

Example B: Imagine that you are having surgery with general anesthesia in an outpatient surgical facility.

A. During the surgery, you were for all intents and purposes unconscious. You heard nothing. Thankfully, you felt nothing. You smelled nothing. You saw nothing, not even light. You were not dreaming or thinking. It was just black—a void. You were not even aware you were alive.

B. Then you move from the operating room to recovery and start to come out of the anesthesia a little bit. At one point, you may come to the surface and be vaguely aware that someone is talking to you. You can hear the voice, and know someone is talking, but have no idea what is being said as you go back under.

C. The next time you come out of anesthesia, you may hear

voices around you and actually understand what they are saying. For example, after one of my surgeries, I came to briefly and heard my surgeon ask why I was still unconscious. A nurse responded, "It's the dilaudid." I went right back under but remembered the comment.

D. Imagine that the next time you come to in the recovery room, someone asks you to put your clothes on to go home. You are still pretty flaccid and out of it, but you become conscious enough to realize you are supposed to be helping someone dress you. You respond to verbal commands with no real understanding of what the words mean. You tell someone your own name, the date, and that George Bush is President, without a clue that you are even speaking. Then, you become vaguely aware of being put into a wheelchair and wheeled outside to a waiting car. You do not presently know why you need to put your clothes on, who the people are asking you to do it, or why you are being put into a car via wheelchair.

E. As your spouse drives you home, the cool air of an open window pulls you conscious enough to realize you are going home from surgery. You know you have had surgery but feel no pain. You understand your spouse is driving because you are still under the influence of anesthesia. You do not really care.

F. When you arrive home, you sleep for hours. Finally, the anesthesia wears off. You become fully conscious. You know who you are, where you are, and what happened to you. You are hungry and able to interact with others normally.

Who, or what part of you, experienced each of these levels of consciousness?

Discussion: Each paragraph, A through F, describes a different level of awareness that you experienced as a result of the effects of drugs on your body.

Level A. During surgery, when you were unconscious and unaware that you were alive, you experienced the level of existence of perhaps a plant or other inanimate object. A plant exists, just as your body existed during surgery. A plant interacts with its environment just as your body interacted with its environment. For example, someone cut pieces out of you. Someone else took your blood pressure, checked your heart rate, and monitored your breathing. Your body was alive and interacting with its environment, but did not know it any more than the plant would know it. Both are alive and undergoing biological processes, though both lack awareness of life. This is a level of consciousness the body experiences from time to time, such as during surgery, when asleep, or after head trauma.

Level B. When you were in the recovery room, you began another level of awareness: one where you knew you were interacting with the environment, and that there was a "you," and a "them," but nothing more. This is a low level of self-awareness, perhaps that of a nonhuman animal.[14]

Maybe a nurse asked, "Can you move your toes?" And you did in fact move your toes. Your body responded to that question without thinking. It just moved the toes in response to the voice, though "you" were not aware of what it was doing. That may be an animal level of awareness, where it responds to an outside stimulus without being aware of its significance. The animal may not understand that there has been an interaction with something outside itself.

Level C. Once you could understand what the voices around you were saying, you reached a third and higher level of awareness. In my own case example, I was aware that people were talking around me, as well as what they were saying. I was aware of my environment to the extent that I realized I was not alone. Most importantly, I was aware that the people were talking about me. That means I was aware that I exist, that I am a person, and that the voices were from different people. But that was the extent of my self-awareness. I did not know who I was, what was going on around me, or why I was there. But I had a level of consciousness that allowed me to comprehend my separate beingness. This might be the level of awareness of a child before he/she reaches what we call "the age of reason." I could not respond to the voices any more than a baby could, but I at least knew that separate beings were involved and that they were relating to me.

Level D. At the time the nurses were dressing you and moving you via wheelchair, you had a fourth and higher level of self-awareness. Doctors call this "oriented times three," meaning a patient is aware of person, place, and time. You were cognizant of your beingness to the point that you could respond knowingly and willingly to other people and their verbal commands, though without having a deep understanding of why. This might be the level of awareness at which some people live. They do things by rote. They do as they are told. They do not think deeply about the why of it. "It's just the way it is," might be their answer if asked why they behave as they do.

Level E. The level of awareness experienced in the car on the way home would be another level at which many humans function. You realized what was going on around you and the why of so much of it as pertained to you. You recognized your mental impairment, much as you would if you had had too much to drink or had used recreational drugs. In other words, you could distinguish your present condition from what is normal for you. You were analytical to that extent. Yet, the drugs, especially the morphine, prevented you from caring about your own well being.

Level F. Once you were completely awake, the medical profession would say you were fully conscious and functioning normally. Your memories returned. You understood everything going on. You cared that the surgery went well. You cared about being hungry and wanted to take care of your body. This is the level of awareness most healthy adult humans experience regularly.

Before reading this example, you most likely believed you were capable of experiencing only two levels of awareness: being awake and being asleep. Now you can see that we are capable of at least six consciousness levels under certain circumstances. Coming out of anesthesia creates the opportunity for experiencing multiple sequential levels of awareness. Coming out of a deep sleep or coma would present other opportunities. And, although we move through awareness levels in sequence as surgical drugs wear off, each level has always existed at the same time within us. We can visit them at will, with or without the assistance of drugs or alcohol. Our Light Being nature allows us to go into each layer and experience it for brief periods of time through focusing our attention and intention.

Other levels of awareness exist beyond, and more expansive than, just the six discussed here. Those of us who have had near-death experiences have enjoyed much higher levels of awareness by going into the Light and starting through the death transformation process. Some people learn to reach higher awareness levels by getting out-of-body. But that is not necessary. We can all learn to use meditation or another form of concentration to experience higher mental states while we are still in the body.

Now that you have convinced yourself that you may have more than two levels of awareness, it is time to explore other levels and their perspectives. You will need only two tools to begin: observing and listening. Try the following exercises to see if you can hear your Light Being self speak.

✳   ✳   ✳

Exercise 2: Relax in a comfortable environment. Form the intention to allow yourself as spirit, soul, or Energy Being, to speak to you. Go through the mental motions of opening your heart to Source's unconditional love. Actually visualize yourself opening up with love. Relax your chest. Breathe deeply and regularly. Relax as though you were going to go to sleep. Still your mind's little voice. And wait. Listen.

✳   ✳   ✳

Exercise 3: Take a walk in comfortable shoes, preferably outside on a sunny day. Start walking at a pace that feels comfortable with your breathing. You do not want to get winded, so do not run. Breathe in a rhythm that matches your walking. For example, inhale while you take three steps and then exhale over five steps. Get into a pattern of breathing and walking in unison. Count steps in your head until the rhythm comes naturally. Then let go. Let your mind go, but do not think. Keep the synchronicity of breathing and stepping for as long as you can. Keep your mind empty. Wait. Listen.

✳   ✳   ✳

Exercise 4: Notice if at any time during the day a thought just seems to "pop" into your mind when you are busy doing something unrelated to the thought. Sometimes this happens in the shower, or when your hands are busy doing something that does not require your concentration. Write down the thought.

* * *

Exercise 5: Just before you go to bed tonight form the intention to communicate with yourself on your Energy Being level of consciousness in your dreams. Ask all of the Light Beings around you to assist in forming a communication link to your own Energy still in the Light. If you have deceased parents or grandparents on whom you often depended while they were alive, ask them to send you Energy to reach that higher vibration where communication can take place. Then sleep and dream. Watch what happens. If you see or hear what seems to be a message, write it down or dictate it so that you will have it when you awaken.

* * *

Discussion: During exercises 2 through 5, eventually a thought entered your mind. Your task now is to determine the nature of the thought and the level of awareness from which it came. The "voice" you heard may have sounded exactly like the voice you always hear in your head when you are thinking—your body's voice. Some people do hear someone else's voice when they communicate with spirit, but do not expect that to happen.

Now the discernment begins. Review the thought and

determine whether it is mundane, meaning it has to do with everyday life in a common or routine way. For example, if while showering, the thought popped into your head that you have to go to the grocery store, that would be a mundane thought. Any thought that reminds you to do some ordinary task should be characterized as mundane. It is possible for our higher levels of awareness to bring us mundane messages. For right now, though, look for something out of the ordinary.

If the thought is not a routine reminder, or prompt to do something ordinary, examine it further. How did it feel to you? Familiar? Exciting? Try to identify the very first emotion associated with the thought, not the one that settled in once you realized its repercussions. For example, the thought could have been, "Suzy is cheating on her math quiz." You have no way of knowing that from home. Your initial emotion might have been anger that your child would cheat. Next, you might have felt excitement that you received a truly insightful message from Universal Knowledge, or denial that the message was valid. If your first reaction signaled you believed the message, such as anger would indicate, then you may well have received a "knowing."

Is the thought an idea you have had before or a new insight or understanding? Does it answer a question you have been mulling over for days, such as what to get Johnny for Christmas, or does it feel like a discovery? Receiving answers to questions we have been pondering for some time may result from the human brain working through a logical analysis, rather than a true message from higher levels of awareness.

A communication via dream may be visual or auditory, or even just a feeling. You might see your deceased parent to whom you prayed for assistance with the exercise. Or you may hear your son's voice during the dream even though he is in Iraq. Perhaps someone in your dream with the face of one person will feel like he/she is someone else you know. For example, a character with the face of a TV star felt like your brother.

Examine the dream communication in a similar way. If you heard a voice, was it out of context with what you were dreaming? Did someone appear in a dream for a brief moment out of sync with the storyline of the dream? How did you feel when you saw the person? How did you feel when you awoke to record the dream? Did you feel someone was trying to give you a message?

✳   ✳   ✳

The above exercises demonstrate that we are innately capable of raising our level of awareness. It is not *necessary* that we do so. We entered into human life specifically to experience its reduced levels of consciousness. So there is no shame in holding fast to human perspective despite others' attempts to expand our horizons.

However, if we seek enlightenment, if our goal is to enjoy as much of our innate spiritual nature as possible while here, we may wish to experience higher levels of perspective. But beware. Raising one's level of awareness can result in changes in attitudes. We may learn that some of our most cherished beliefs are backwards. More importantly, we may discover that our entire view of reality has shifted, tearing a hole in our beliefs as surely as an earthquake opens fissures in the earth.

Think back to the example of the six levels of awareness possible during surgery and recovery. Each sensation was real for so long as it lasted. Each level of awareness was a valid experience. Yet consciousness shifted from one level to another as the body awakened from the anesthesia. The body woke up.

The same thing happens when we raise our awareness to a higher level. *We souls* wake up. We transition through various levels of enlightenment until we are fully aware that we are Beings of Light who have allowed part of our consciousness to "sleep" and "dream" of being human. Eventually, we will know for a fact that we have never been separate beings at all. We have always been one of many facets of Source's own personality and self-awareness.

Human Perspective	Light Being Perspective	Source's Perspective
I wake up when I leave the sleep state.	My soul Energy wakes up when it realizes I am a Light Being, not a human.	My Light Beings wake up when they realize they are me.

Stepping up a level of perspective can open us up to the love and joy that envelope us in the Light. We will understand that this experience is not all there is to life. So, the consequences of our decisions and actions take on less significance. We can enjoy the wonderful and challenging aspects of human life without worrying ourselves to death about every event or decision.

6
✳ Who's In Charge?

WHEN PART OF OUR Light Being Energy enters into a human before birth to become its soul, it does not *take over* the human. We know this because people would behave much more lovingly if souls were able to control human lives.

What happens is the two species, body and soul, are blended together. Their levels of awareness, personalities, emotions, and innate natures meld. Sometimes these different innate natures conflict with each other. What results is an internal struggle over which being will control our lives. The cartoon of a devil on one shoulder and angel on the other comes to mind.

In general, most of us allow human nature to govern behavior. In fact, we have structured our societies around human character traits. Each level of government employs police forces and houses inmates in prisons and jails in acknowledgement of mankind's innate violence. The fact that we have massive military ranks reflects the human inclinations toward possessiveness, territoriality, and protectiveness of self and family. Governments, businesses, schools, and even social organizations, have hierarchical structures because humans are competitive and structure their "herds" according to dominance traits. Thousands of churches are founded on the human fear of death and belief in divine retribution.

There is nothing inherently wrong with how human societies are structured. The constant emphasis on human traits, however, reinforces our erroneous assumption that we ourselves are human. So we blindly continue to limit ourselves to human beliefs, human thoughts, and human abilities, when we could be so much more.

The importance of the fact that we are Light Being souls is that our behavior need not be restricted by or to human traits. We have separate and distinct Light Being innate personality attributes we can study, develop, and prize. How can we tell which personality traits belong to our spiritual identity?

Certainly our eternal personalities have been greatly influenced by years of human life. Yet, we can learn to distinguish some marked differences between the two personalities so that we may consciously choose which one we will allow to control our behavior in any given situation.

Humans share, to varying degrees, the following innate traits: fear, which makes them controlling, self-centered, and resistant to change; and competitiveness, which renders man anxious about his relative status in society. Humans are possessive and jealous, violent and revengeful, playful and lazy. One of the most prevalent and destructive human traits is they are judgmental. On the other hand, humans can be fiercely loyal, protective of others, and sometimes heroic. They have been known to sacrifice their lives to save others, especially family and friends.

Light Being innate traits include creativity, compassion, and curiosity. We are unconditionally loving, accepting, and egalitarian. Our intelligence and self-awareness far exceeds anything a human can hope to attain. On the other hand, Light Beings' are so non-judgmental that we have no sense of discretion or discernment.

Which nature would most likely come to the forefront in the following situations?

＊　　＊　　＊

Question 1:　You are a physician specializing in internal medicine. You have worked for three long years to build your patient base to be large enough to generate sufficient revenue to support your spouse and small children. During college you joined the National Guard for its education benefits and to learn how to fly. Now the Guard has called you up to serve in Iraq. What is your instinctive reaction to this news?

Discussion: *Human perspective*: Your initial reaction will very likely be human because the idea of going to war automatically triggers the fight-flight-freeze chemical reaction in the hindbrain. You probably will experience fear of being killed in action, dread, and a sense of being trapped in a situation from which you cannot safely extricate yourself. You must report for duty or suffer the consequences, which could include confinement in a military prison.

After the instantaneous emotional reaction already described recedes, human animal nature might dictate a self-preservation and protection of the family response. You have struggled through twelve years of medical training, and three years of practice, to get to the point where you can support your family. Your children and patients need you. You have sacrificed greatly to get where you are, and have taken more than your fair share of indigent patients as a community service. You know that if you are gone for more than a few months, you will lose most of your patients to whomever fills in for you. You will have to devote considerable time rebuilding your practice when you return from Iraq. How can you put your family through that again?

Alternatively, human feelings of loyalty and duty could arise. You may reason that it is every American's responsibility to serve this country. You signed a contract when you joined the National Guard that you would report to active duty if called. America needs both doctors and pilots in Iraq. Terrorism must be stopped. You will go and defend your way of life.

Light Being perspective. Instantly reacting to this news from the Light Being level would be the rarest of occurrences. Few of us could hear that we are going to war and react with peace and acceptance. Light Beings are completely non-judgmental and accepting of anything occurring in human life. So, serving as either a medical officer or as a pilot would be acceptable at this level of perspective because going to Iraq would lead to a wealth of human emotional experiences.

Soul perspective: The soul is often called the "conscience" of the human being. We souls have gained wisdom over the course of living many, many lives and experiencing the same situation from different vantage points.

You probably would not have a clearly identifiable spiritual response to the assignment to active duty. Instead, many conflicting thoughts and emotions may be generated at the soul level because of the interplay between human and Light Being personalities. You may also have unhealed traumas from other lives that you have carried over into this one that affect how you feel about war. Your reaction might change depending upon whether the Guard would require you to serve as a doctor, helping those wounded in combat, or as a pilot, bombing living beings. Consequently, you may try to find a way to limit military service to medical care, as opposed to flying.

Ultimately, your job is to mediate the emotional tug-of-war and help guide the decision to one that you can live with from a practical standpoint.

✳ ✳ ✳

Question 2: Your family has for generations lived on a plot of land in the part of New Orleans below sea level, in one of the "hollows" in West Virginia, on a Pacific Coast Highway hillside, or at the base of Mount St. Helens. You love your homeland. All of your childhood memories flow around its grass, trees, buildings, and patch of sky. You want your children to share those memories and add their own. But one day Hurricane Katrina wipes out your New Orleans flat. A huge thunderstorm washes out the hillside of your West Virginia hollow, pushing your house downhill. Torrential rains create a mudslide that slips your home across Pacific Coast Highway toward the Ocean. Or Mount St. Helens belches out toxic gases and cinders that light your house afire.

What is your reaction? Do you rebuild on the same land? Why?

Discussion: *Human perspective*. One would think that pure animal nature decides this question. Animals instinctively avoid known dangers. The human survival instinct should lead you to relocate to safer ground.

But your human reaction might be to rebuild even though the property has been proven uninhabitable. After Hurricane Katrina, the news was rife with stories about people who returned to their former homes to rebuild on land known to be susceptible to flooding. Humans, like other animals, are innately territorial, and, once having staked out their ground, will defend it against all comers. Humans are also reluctant to change, and so may continue a pattern set earlier in their own lives or those of their parents. If moving is not financially feasible, the survival instinct may lead you to stay where a homestead is affordable and to try to shield it from further damage.

Light Being perspective. Again, few of us would respond to this situation from the Light Being perspective. At the purely spiritual level, we know that land cannot in fact be owned. We recognize that Earth is a collective manifestation. It would not matter then whether we decided to stay or move. Light Beings are not judgmental by nature. Any choice would be acceptable because it would lead to experiences. That is the purpose of assuming the human role.

Soul perspective. What may ultimately cause us to rebuild on unsuitable land, and generate intense conflict over "making the right decision," is the confusion contributed to the decision-making process by the soul. Your soul personality blends human animal and Light Being traits from this lifetime, as well as many others. Complex emotions and motivations garnered during your hundreds or thousands of years of living as different people get layered atop current life experiences. Your belief that you need to stay on the right path will also tug at your spiritual heart.

You may be caught up in feelings of loyalty, fondness, and/or fear that you will not be able to afford another place. You may suffer feelings of abandonment, loss, protectiveness, guilt, or remorse. You may unconsciously be dealing with a wide-range of concerns. Maybe you heard your own grandfather say many times that he wanted his grandchildren to live on the land handed down through generations of his family. Perhaps you have a strong desire to stay close to other family members. You may have a deeply held but unremembered belief that you intended to experience this type of loss, perhaps more than once, to study how your responses to multiple living displacements would evolve. At the heart of the matter may be layers upon layers of pain. The emotional baggage we all pull along with us can include a desire for revenge against nature carried over from another lifetime, or a generalized anger over the unfairness of life.

We must identify and sort through all our emotions, some of which we may not understand because we do not remember the experiences that created them, in order to know ourselves—in order to make a decision that works for the human we inhabit and enhances our own evolution as well. We may have to examine all possible reactions and options and come to a decision we feel is logical, rather than purely emotional.

For example, would it not make a difference to know that your devotion to the land was originally formed in childhood, hearing your grandfather say over and over that he believes family should live on family land? What if your grandfather has moved into a condo several states away, suggesting he no longer feels that strongly about the land? Perhaps your emotional attachment to the homestead should have moved on when your grandfather did.

Or, as another example, would you still rebuild on dangerous ground if you knew that your connection to it was formed in another lifetime, say as an American Indian driven westward from that same piece of property? Maybe it is time to finally heal that wound.

Every choice we face can be analyzed in the same way from different perspectives *if* we have the awareness to do so. This exercise might demonstrate how different our choices could be if examined in the glare of enlightenment.

✳   ✳   ✳

Question 3: One plot of the TV show *Cold Case* revolved around four brothers, three of whom were killed one after the other in a feud over the youngest brother's scooter. The local Chicano gang leader who stole the scooter shot the oldest brother for trying to recover it. The second brother was killed in a shoot out he initiated to avenge the first brother's death. The third was killed the same way. Yet the youngest brother still felt honor bound to seek revenge. He said, "My brothers' deaths are on my back."

What would you decide? From which level of awareness are you making that decision?

Discussion: *Human perspective.* Human beings seem to be the only animals to engage in revenge. In the rest of the animal world, when a dispute arises two combatants fight it out until one is dominant. Emotions and drives dissipate during the battle. The foes part ways. Rarely does a black bear seek revenge against the winner of a fight. Other animals generally do not carry on feuds between bloodlines, as did the notorious Hatfield and McCoy human families. Can you imagine a wolf killing off all the chickens on a farm because the farmer maimed a member of his pack with his tractor?

Revenge is a response to intense pain, nearly always emotional pain. The pain of being violated, offended, or humiliated can be highly motivating. So you might well decide to avenge your brothers' deaths if you acted from human nature.

Light Being perspective. Light Beings do not judge or condemn. Any choice would be understood, even murder, because it would lead to experience, which is the purpose of entering human life. Eventually, after witnessing revenge from all angles, you would complete your study of it as a human experience and move on to other themes in subsequent lifetimes.

Soul perspective. As a Light Being soul, you carry the unconscious memories of other lifetimes' experiences that may color your reactions to this situation. They give you context and insight unavailable to the human being. For example, you might conclude that your parents have suffered enough and should not be subjected to the loss of yet another son. Your intellectual nature might lead you to a practical decision: retaliation will not bring back the dead. Nor will it give you peace of mind.

* * *

Question 4: You are driving down the freeway on your way to a very important meeting. You are running late. The meeting cannot start without you, perhaps because it is a parent-teacher conference, or because you are chairing the meeting. Important people who do not like to wait are being held up. You will look irresponsible and unorganized if you are late. You do not want other people to have that impression of you. So, you are speeding, keeping one eye on the road and the other roaming the countryside looking for highway patrol cars. Another car comes out of nowhere and cuts you off, preventing you from getting off the freeway at your exit.

What is your *first* impulse? What action do you take?

Discussion: *Human perspective*. Your first impulse is typically going to be human. You curse because you are stressed and angry. Then you give the guy the finger as you race by him on your way to the next exit. Why are these emotions and behaviors so common and understandable in our lives? Because we normally allow our human's personality to run our lives, and anger is an innate human trait. So is competitiveness.

In this instance, the human animal instinct is to feel competitive, and indeed thwarted, in the struggle for dominance. You were lead dog in the race up the freeway before you were cut off. The intruder asserted his superiority over you by redirecting you from your goal. Your body's animal instinct was to feel competitive when challenged by a more aggressive animal. You lost the initial competition as you watched your exit receding in the rearview mirror. Animal instinct then drove you, and literally drove your car, to speed up to try to reassert yourself by passing the challenger. You gave him the one-finger salute as a sign of dominance over him, because otherwise he may not have even known he was in competition with you. The gesture was a victory dance as well, reaffirming your Alpha dog status in your own mind.

Does any of this sound familiar? Does any of it have anything whatsoever to do with you as the soul personality? It might.

Soul perspective. While the impulse and action described above originally arose purely from the animal's personality, this is definitely not the first time you have encountered similar challenges to your dominance over the material world. Each time we souls experience events of this nature, and our bodies' animal responses to them, it makes an indelible imprint upon our eternal personalities. Years of such experiences can overtake our Light Being character and form an emotional and behavioral habit that we carry over from one human lifetime to the next—until healed.

Eventually, like today, we may find ourselves getting angry, cursing, and giving the finger to just about anybody on the road whose behavior somehow strikes us wrong. We call it road rage when the behavior escalates into violence. But even these small, unseen acts of anger and defiance are road rage because they are disproportionate to the injury suffered. The cursing and finger jabbing may well have been fueled by many unrelated events from your past, rather than the one little incident on the way to today's meeting.

Light Being perspective. What would be the Light Being level of perspective on this situation? We would recognize the event for what it is. The other driver was simply moving faster than we were and wanted into the right hand lane for reasons of his own. The Light Being does not judge his actions. It merely observes them. The situation requires no response other than to get to the next exit, turn off the highway, and double back to the area where the meeting will be held. It would be a courtesy to call ahead and announce an unexpected late arrival.

$$* \quad * \quad *$$

These exercises show that often our host bodies will provide the initial emotional reactions and responses to an event. Our own reactions as souls will not surface until we have had an opportunity to distance ourselves from the onslaught of human passions. Understanding this sequence of emotional eruptions, and the basic natures and motivations of the two beings within one body, gives us a foundation for growth. We can learn to wait until our bodies' tempers have cooled before making decisions. We can then focus our attention and intention on shifting our perspectives to a higher level to choose how to behave.

Human Perspective	Light Being Perspective	Source's Perspective
I do what is in my own best interests with little concern for others.	That part of me serving as a soul will adopt many human traits that I will have to reverse through reconditioning with unconditional love.	What makes human life interesting for me is the complex interplay between human and Light Being traits.

7

✳ What Is And Isn't Unconditional Love

WE EACH BELIEVE WE recognize love when we experience it. But that belief reflects only that we have been exposed to behavior called "love." We have been trained to associate the word love with how our parents related to one another, how we were raised, how family members have interacted, and how potential mates have treated us. Was any of that behavior really love? Think through the following exercises to discover how well you have been trained to recognize true unconditional love.

✳   ✳   ✳

Exercise 1: Match the common male-female relationship practice or concept on the left with its characterization on the right.

1. "Friends with benefits"   A. Acting on the sex drive

2. Engagement   B. Cultural reflection of once legal promise

3. Asking a woman's brother, ex-boyfriend, or father if he is "OK" with you dating her

C. Recognition of another male's dominance; respect

4. Marriage

D. Lifestyle and legal rights

5. "Hooking up"

E. Acting on the sex drive

6. A man paying for dinner and expecting at least a kiss at the end of the night, if not sex

F. Manipulation, control and dominance

7. Having multiple sexual partners at the same time

G. Acting on the sex drive

8. A woman withholding sex to get what she wants from a mate

H. Manipulation, control and dominance

Discussion: Obviously, or maybe not so obviously, this was a trick exercise. The practices and concepts on the left are already matched with their characterization as love or other motivation on the right. Note that none of these commonly accepted rituals of dating and mating reflect true love of the other person from the Light Being level of perspective. Some of them probably seem like love from the soul's vantage point, such as engagement and marriage, but their true nature may be something entirely different. Analyze each one of these practices from the three levels of perspective of human nature, soul personality as it has been affected by multiple human lifetimes, and Light Being nature.

1. *Friends with benefits.* If you are not in touch with high school and college-aged people, you may not be familiar with the term "friends with benefits." It means having a sexual relationship with someone who is a friend or buddy for whom one has no romantic feelings. In other words, the parties admittedly do not "love" each other.

Half of this relationship is obviously based upon the sex drive, as indicated by the "with benefits" phrase. Whether there is true sexual attraction or not may depend upon the two participants. Some of these arrangements may fulfill raw animal nature only, particularly among those who believe that the male sex drive needs as much attention as eating and drinking.

The question becomes whether the "friends" half of the arrangement satisfies something from the soul's perspective. The answer would depend upon how well the two have communicated their true intentions to one another.

If the parties mutually agree that they want to have sexual relations though neither has a romantic interest in the other, then all is well, even from the Being of Light's perspective. Enjoying another's company in many ways is part of the reason we choose to become human. Unconditional love is a possibility in this type relationship because the parties have abandoned the stereotypical judgments that often accompany sexual relationships.

If, however, one party is deluding him/herself about his/her own true feelings about the other, or the arrangement, then emotional pain can result. The relationship degenerates from being potentially unconditionally loving to causing emotional harm.

2. Engagement and 4. Marriage. Wedding industry advertising would have us believe a marriage proposal is the epitome of romantic love. Marriage is so valued in most modern societies that laws are enacted to create and protect it. Legal battles are fought to define it. Does this legal connection provide a clue as to marriage's true nature? It is considered a contract by law. Marriage confers all types of legal status, including rights of inheritance, community property rights, support rights and obligations, and child rearing rights and obligations. Do these legal principles have anything to do with love? If love were a requirement for marriage, there could be no legal unions between U.S. citizens and foreign nationals who marry to avoid deportation, or between mail-order brides and their spouses. As the song claims, "what's love got to do with it?"

Beyond the legal status they confer, engagement and marriage are lifestyle choices and cultural norms. This may be what appeals to human nature. Humans are herd animals and most often follow established behavior patterns. The history of marriage is also replete with periods of treating women as possessions, something that may appeal to the animal drive for dominance.

The soul personality has probably been steeped in the marriage tradition over multiple lifetimes and has come to regard it as a

WHAT IS AND ISN'T UNCONDITIONAL LOVE

normal expression of human love. Unconditional love might be possible in marriage, but the arrangement itself is structured as an exchange of services, not love. (This is discussed in detail in *BACKWARDS Love*, the next book in this series to be published.)

From the Light Being level of awareness, engagement and marriage are irrelevant. They are outward signs indicative of Earth life. Nothing more. Love, true love from the Light Being soul is an innate character trait, not an outward display or living arrangement.

3. *Getting clearance to pursue a woman.* Asking a father for his daughter's hand in marriage is an old-fashioned custom rarely used today. What may still exist is one male asking another for clearance to pursue a female with whom the other male has/had a relationship. This can take the form of, "Hey Bob, is it alright if I date your sister?" to, "Dog, you got no problem with my hookin' up with your ex, right?" Any and all versions of this ritual arise from the animal perspective of male dominance—showing respect to another male, and, at the same time, regarding the female as a possession rather than a person.

Neither the soul nor the Light Being can relate to this custom because of its implied possessiveness. Unconditional love is not possessive.

5. *Hooking up.* "Hooking up" may be similar to what the older among us call "a one night stand," although the term hooking up is sometimes used for any type of sexual encounter in any context. The difference between "hooking up" and "friends with benefits"

may lie in the level of sexual attraction involved. Alcohol and drugs sometimes figure prominently in hooking up. So does the sex drive. Love does not. Hooking up is pure animal behavior. However, that does not mean it is repugnant to the Light Being or soul.

One of the more startling discoveries of my sojourn in the Light was that sex for enjoyment's sake is perfectly acceptable from a spiritual viewpoint. In fact, it is one of the reasons we choose to spend time in a physical body. True to their non-judgmental nature, Light Beings see sex as no more, and no less, than a physical instinct. Humans are the ones who have constructed taboos around sex, based upon purely human notions of what is right and wrong.

6. *Sex in exchange for dinner.* The notion of a man paying for dinner and expecting sexual favors at the end of the evening is now cliché because dating and mating rituals have changed dramatically. Yet some version of the notion persists in many males. It even invades male expectations of marriage. Some men believe they have the right to manipulate a woman, make her feel guilty and beholden, because they have spent money on her. This type of logic is more animal cunning than reason. It arises from the human instinct to dominate.

From the soul perspective, this particular dating ritual might be tolerated if childhood training or observations misled the man or woman into believing it is acceptable behavior. Yet underlying that acceptability for the woman may well be suppressed hurt, anger, and despair, because this conduct devalues a woman and robs her of her innate equality.

The Light Being does not judge dating practices any more than it judges any other behavior. However, if one person's actions cause pain for the other, the underlying motivations remove the situation from one of consensual physical gratification. In this situation, if the woman feels devalued because the man believes he has purchased access to her body by paying for dinner, then the resulting emotional hurt makes any sexual conduct unacceptable. Or, if the man in fact believes he has purchased sexual favors even though the woman is not a prostitute, then his sense of entitlement taints any physical contact. Sex is only beautiful and natural when both partners openly welcome it.

7. *Multiple sexual partners.* Generally, this activity has nothing to do with love and reflects animal drives. But that does not necessarily mean it is inconsistent with Light Being nature. Again, as spiritual beings, we cherish enjoyment of all the physical body has to offer. The only caveat we would attach would be that we should demonstrate consideration and respect for ourselves and our sexual partners by taking steps to prevent disease and unwanted pregnancy, making certain both parties have the same intention, and treating each other with respect and kindness instead of greed and inconsideration.

8. *Using sex to manipulate.* A woman who uses sex to manipulate a man is doing the same thing as the man who uses money to garner sexual favors. Manipulation is an animal behavior. From the

higher perspective of the Light Being, this type of conduct does not show love, even if there is love between the two partners. Manipulation is a control mechanism, and our spiritual nature dictates that we have no right to control another's life or choices for any reason.

✳   ✳   ✳

Exercise 2: Acceptance of which of the following demonstrates unconditional love? Allowing your child to:

A. get tattoos

B. dye his/her hair pink, purple, or multi-colors

C. wear his/her hair in corn rows, spiked out with hair gel, in dread locks, or some fantastic hair style

D. adopt a "Goth" appearance

E. pierce multiple body locations and wear earrings in them

F. use lip plates to expand lip size or put a bone through his/her nose

G. cut his/her arms and legs to make himself/herself "feel alive"

H. cut off an ear lobe, part of a finger, or other appendage to look "different"

I. use abusive language toward you

J. drink or use drugs

Discussion: A parent's role is to rear children to function in human society. It is part of animal nature. Most of the listed activities do not further the goal of training a child to fit into herd norms. So permitting these behaviors would not be considered love at the human level.

Some of the behaviors relate to a child's Light Being creativity and self-expression, such as choices A. through E. Unconditional love demands that the child not be judged for appearance choices and be accepted for who he/she is despite fashions offensive to the parents' and the human herd's tastes.

Other choices are more body mutilation than style, like F through H, and J. When a child starts damaging his/her host body, through conduct listed above or by overeating, not getting enough sleep, anorexia, or bulimia, it is an indication of suppressed pain and must be investigated. Self-destructive behaviors are more about the child's emotional health than they are an indication of personal preference. Unconditional love does not mean accepting all behaviors regardless of consequences.

Accepting abusive language from a child may simply reflect the fatigue that results from constantly monitoring and correcting behavior. That is understandable. But the child should be made to understand the difference between cursing to vent anger or frustration and verbal abuse directed personally at a parent to cause hurt. The motivations for true parent abuse should be investigated and handled accordingly.

*   *   *

Exercise 3: When it comes to choosing a mate, which of the following characteristics relate to (1) human animal perspective, (2) soul personality, and (3) Light Being perspective?

A. Great sense of humor

B. Good health

C. Devotion to parents and their well being

D. Ability to work through conflict with understanding

E. Deep religious beliefs

F. Loves sports and athletic activities

G. Loves children

H. Earns a good living to support a family

I. Musical or artistic talents

J. Volunteers time and money to charity

K. Always tries to do the right thing

L. Physical attractiveness

Discussion: You may have divided the list into categories 1, 2, and 3 depending upon how you understand the three levels of awareness. That is exactly what this exercise requests. Yet, at the outset we must acknowledge that mating is an entirely animal behavior. Nevertheless, many of the traits are desirable from more than one perspective for different reasons.

a. Humor. A great sense of humor appeals to just about every level of perspective because it reflects joy—the joy of living. Joy is truly a Light Being innate characteristic and should be treasured in everyone.

A sense of humor also suggests a person does not take him/herself so seriously that he/she cannot poke fun at life and his/her own foibles. Someone who takes him/herself or life too seriously tends to have a soul personality riddled with emotional issues that may affect the relationship. That is not necessarily an undesirable trait in a mate. We souls carry over emotional issues from other lives to be resolved in this lifetime, and the mating relationship may provide the opportunity for healing. We may have chosen to mate with a humorless person precisely to observe how we respond to that trait.

b. Health. Humans instinctively seek out mates in good health because it assures propagation of the species. It is an animal survival instinct.

Selecting a mate with less than perfect health may serve the soul's purpose for choosing this lifetime, knowing in advance that the soul intended to experience what it would be like to live with a physically challenged person.

At the Light Being level of awareness, we look through the physical being to the spirit inside. Health is irrelevant.

c. Devotion to parents. Familial or bloodline ties are animal instincts. Yet, during my beyond death experience I was aware of having something like lineage or other form of grouping with my five Light Being friends. My understanding is that we form agreements with other Light Beings to come into human life together to support each other. So, having the trait of devotion to parents can be attractive on all levels.

d. Ability to work through conflict. The ability to gracefully work through conflict is a learned skill. Its presence may well reflect the soul's learning from hundreds of lifetimes. This trait would be attractive to the Light Being and soul levels of awareness.

The human animal would not value this trait much because dispute resolution through violence and/or domination is more its norm.

e. Deep religious beliefs. Your initial reaction may be that having religious beliefs would be attractive at the Light Being level of perspective. My understanding from Universal Knowledge is just the opposite. Religion is a man-made institution born of, and perpetuated through, human fear of death. If a person has deeply held religious beliefs, and is unwilling to hear and consider new ideas or insights from within, then it would seem the person is stuck in a non-growth pattern. Light Beings have an innate character trait of intense curiosity and willingness to grow and experience. We are not attracted to those who refuse self-enlightenment.

Fear-based personality traits appeal to the human, and perhaps the soul personality if it has not evolved enough to escape fear of death and its consequences.

f. Loves sports/athletic activities. All animals engage in recreation. Who has not seen the bear cubs running and playing with each other on National Geographic? So this trait may appeal at the human level. Watching sports alone on TV may be an indication of living at the animal level.

This trait might also appeal to the soul, depending upon the experiences it has chosen for this lifetime. Sharing enjoyable sports and athletic activities could add richness to the fabric of a relationship. Engaging in sports creates opportunities for growth experiences. So might participating in a group that watches the sport.

Sports are attractive from the Light Being perspective, especially if the person actively participates in physical activities instead of just watching someone else. Having experiences of all types is a purpose for living.

g. Loves children. You may immediately exclaim that this trait appeals to the animal nature of our hosts—survival instinct, propagation of the species, and all that. Correct.

Children also appeal to our Light Being level of awareness. We can see in them the joy inherent in our true nature. And their innocence and unconditional love reflect our spiritual side so clearly. Babies' open-ended trust proclaims the oneness we share, the interdependence, and the collective caring.

h. Good provider. Valuing someone for his/her ability to earn a living and provide for a mate and family is a human characteristic.

You knew that.

i. Musical or artistic talents. Unless you chose to mate with an artist or musician in order to experience a certain lifestyle, this trait appeals primarily to the Light Being level because creativity is one of our innate characteristics.

j. Charitable works. The human animal perspective is self-centered. It does not generally care about unrelated others. So this trait probably would not appeal to human nature.

Whether this personality trait relates to the soul or Light Being level of perspective depends upon the potential mate's motivations. Some people use charities to enhance their own self-image. Volunteer work looks good on a résumé. Being publicly recognized for good works strengthens the ego, which is a function of the body/soul combined personality. We must discover why and how the potential mate volunteers time and money to charities before we can discern which level of personality is behind this activity.

k. Always tries to do the "right thing." This one is a trap. The quotation marks around the words "right thing" are the tip off.

The concept of right and wrong is purely human—but not purely animal. Animals generally do not have moral codes. Humans, on the other hand, do have morals because souls' higher levels of awareness intermingle with animal fear of death to generate rules of behavior in an attempt to assure a pathway to immortality. That concern is unfounded. We do not need to follow human-constructed rules of conduct to earn heaven. We are now and will always be part of Source. Our return to what we call heaven is automatic because of our nature as Source.

The habit of trying to do the right thing would appeal most to the body/soul combined personality because of the emotional issues that could be resolved through relating to an individual with this character trait. Who determines what the "right thing" is in any given situation? Right in whose opinion? How are various "rights" weighed against each other? Does the potential mate use his/her "right thing" moral compass to lord it over those perceived as lacking one? Is this just an ego trip that really signals the person thinks he/she is always right? If you mate with a person who always tries to be right, have a good long talk about your respective values and opinions to make certain you are both on the same "right" page.

Light Beings are unique in that they form no judgments. They have no concept of "right or wrong" and so would not value trying to do the "right" thing as a personality trait.

l. Physical attractiveness. Another trap. You think this one is a slam-dunk animal value. It is.

It can also be a Light Being value. Our true nature is so uncompromisingly beautiful that we gravitate to beauty in all its forms. The human physique can be quite beautiful. There is nothing wrong with enjoying it.

The desire to have a physically attractive mate can become a problem when one lacks awareness of why he/she is so attracted to physical beauty. If it is purely sexual, that is the body's animal nature. If we are attracted to physical loveliness, naturally surrounding ourselves with beauty in all its forms like an artist might, we may be reveling in splendor as a Light Being does. If, however, someone seeks out physically attractive potential mates because he/she thinks they enhance his/her own image, he/she is thinking like a human. He/she is using a person as a competitive tool, instead of enjoying a potentially loving relationship.

*   *   *

Chapter 12 of *BACKWARDS: Returning to Our Source for Answers* describes the various emotions and motivations that humans call "love" and compares them to unconditional love. In summary, love is understood differently depending upon level of awareness:

Human Perspective	Light Being Perspective	Source's Perspective
Love is any behavior I call "love."	Unconditional love requires that we do not judge another. It is a state of mind.	Unconditional love is my innate nature.

This table discloses how we can move from the human perspective to higher ones: we must train ourselves to overcome the innate human animal instinct to be judgmental. We then consciously accept that all of creation constitutes Source, and as such is worthy of our love. Repeat as needed. Eventually we will instinctively react from the soul with unconditional love, instead of responding from the human personality with judgment.

Do not, however, confuse unconditional love with condoning bad behavior. We do not have to accept abuse from other people. Nor do we have to continue relationships with those who do not treat us with love and respect. We always have the right to choose what behaviors we will tolerate. We can unconditionally love someone without subjecting ourselves to his/her temperament.

Unconditional love means only that we continue to love a person as part of Source though we might despise his/her conduct at times. It means we have removed from our attitude the judgment that the person is bad, wrong, evil, and unlovable just because he/she does not act as we want him/her to act. Love means not "throwing out the baby with the bathwater." In other words, we do not completely condemn a person for individual undesirable acts.

Unconditional love also does not mean "never having to say you're sorry," as proclaimed in the movie *Love Story*, starring Ali MacGraw and Ryan O'Neal. In fact, just the opposite is true. We should apologize to others when we have treated them with less than unconditional love. That is part of how we train ourselves to behave better in the future. The humility required to say "I'm sorry" helps keep our focus on consideration for other people and away from human self-centeredness.

The whole concept of love in all its forms, from familial to mating, is so complex and so backwards in our current cultures and societies that another *BACKWARDS* book will be devoted to this topic.

8

* Reeducation

MUCH OF OUR ADVERTISING is geared toward physical attractiveness. Beautifying products, ranging from clothing to scents, dominate American advertising. Female sexuality is used to sell everything from automobiles to yachts. Watching television today leaves the impression that the human procreative instinct reigns supreme in our lives. All our emphasis appears to be on our hosts' bodies. There are literally no advertisements on how to make our eternal personalities more attractive. Nor does the advertising industry even acknowledge our existence as souls.

Countries spend billions of dollars to train human brains by filling them with data in what we call "education." At the same time, our societies completely neglect the fact that as souls we can access "knowings" on any subject through contact with Universal Knowledge. No effort is made to assist us in developing this innate talent.

Millions of dollars are spent annually on how to celebrate

weddings as parties, and relatively nothing is spent to preserve the marriages themselves.

All of our focus has been on humans. But we are not humans. We are spiritual beings inhabiting humans. Our lives are forever. Yet our societies are built upon values that die when our hosts do.

Human Perspective	Light Being Perspective	Source's Perspective
The material world is all-important.	Our spiritual nature is all-important.	Both physical and spiritual experiences are important to me.

It is hard enough to raise our spiritual awareness without being constantly bombarded with messages relevant only to our hosts. There is one powerful force in the world that could be harnessed to help us shift our awareness up a level. The media hold tremendous power that could be redirected to remind all of us of our true Light Being nature. Our emphasis could be shifted from temporary beings to eternal ones through a creative ad campaign. Doing so would be much easier than we suspect, as the following exercise discloses.

✳   ✳   ✳

Exercise: See if you can match the following TV commercials with the human, or Light Being, innate characteristic to which it primarily appeals:

1. Teenage boy listening to his iPod and dancing around the kitchen while he waits for his Totino's Pizza Rolls to be cooked in the microwave

   A. The human survival instinct, with a bit of competitiveness

2. Hungry Man frozen dinners commercial where man who eats salad gets blown away by the wind, while man who eats Hungry Man dinner does not

   B. The Light Being trait of creativity

3. The Progressive Insurance commercial with the jingle: "That's the way life should be."

   C. Human sexuality

4. TV commercial where every man driving a car is turned away at his date's door, but the man riding a motor-cycle is invited in for the night

   D. The Light Being's inner joyfulness over experiencing a small aspect of physical life

5. Target Store's ad showing various products which morph into other products related by shape or color

   F. The Light Being tendency to be helpful rather than competitive

Discussion: This exercise demonstrates how products can be represented in ways that either appeal to our innate Light Being nature or to our bodies' animal nature.

TV commercial 1 matches with D. The boy revels in the joy of music as he fixes his snack, the consumption of which will be another joyful experience. It is also noteworthy that the young man cooks his own pizza rolls, instead of asking his mother to do it. Some commercials hide a subliminal message of male dominance over women. An example is the Bounty paper towel commercial where a man and his son try to guess how many sheets of paper toweling would be required for the wife to clean up a spill. The men make no attempt to clean it up themselves.

Commercial 2 matches with choice A because it plays up competition between men, while at the same time it implies survival is at stake if a man eats a lighter meal. These are both purely human concerns.

Commercial 3 matches with choice F. The text of the commercial is that Progressive Insurance Company's website provides insurance quotes for its competitors to compare with its own quote, allowing the consumer to exercise free will in making a choice. While clearly the ad is about the competitiveness of Progressive's rates, which relates to a human instinct, it can also be viewed as educational—satisfying the consumer's curiosity about market rates. And, curiosity is definitely a Light Being trait.

Commercial 4 obviously relates to choice C because of the dating context. The commercial plays on a man's sense of masculinity by implying that a motorcycle arouses a woman's sexual interest while a car does not. This is clearly human animal oriented.

Commercial 5 demonstrates choice B. The Source-given creativity of the artists who designed the ad clearly shows not only in the morphing technology but also in the relationships between the objects from which, and into which, the products morph.

One of my favorite TV commercials is produced by Liberty Mutual Insurance Company. The ad features several people instinctively helping others, and ends with the tag line, "When it's people helping each other, they call it acting responsibly. When an insurance company does it, it's called Liberty Mutual." In the opening scene, a woman physically restrains a young man to the curb to prevent him from being hit by a car. Another scene shows a kitchen worker helping a woman reach a pot on a shelf over her head. A third has a woman kicking a basketball back to kids playing in their driveway, so that they do not chase it into oncoming traffic. This short film clip highlights the Light Being traits of oneness, looking out for one another, joyful service to each other, and unconditional love.

As these TV commercials demonstrate, small visual and sound bites have major impact in reinforcing or tearing down societal stereotypes. Each additional reinforcement helps cement human habits into place. While we are trying to change our perspectives, and grow into more awareness of our spirituality, it would be wonderful if the same types of visual and auditory reinforcements film/characters!

could be available to us. Ads could continuously remind us to be kind, loving, accepting, joyful, and thoughtful. Used in this way, mass media can be an effective tool for shifting our awareness away from animal nature toward Light Being nature in order to raise the consciousness levels of everyone on Earth.

9

Self-Healing

THE HUMAN BODY HAS built-in repair mechanisms that allow it to heal. You may have heard about stem cells because of the controversy surrounding their use in medical research. Stem cells retain the embryonic ability to differentiate into any type of tissue the body needs to repair itself, including organs. "At all stages of your life, your body responds to damage by recruiting stem cells. When you smoke, stem cells are sent to the lungs to respond to damage. Or when your skin burns from the sun, stem cells go there to make repairs," according to the Oprah Winfrey Show's Dr. Mehmet Oz.[15]

Whether we are able to take full advantage of our bodies' self-healing skills depends upon whether we believe in them. We souls manifest what we truly believe about ourselves into the physical reality of our human hosts. If we reject the truth of self-healing, that belief may overwrite our bodies' physiology.

Ask yourself now whether you believe humans can heal themselves.

✳   ✳   ✳

Question 1: Do you believe your body can heal itself?

Discussion: Of course you do! You have seen it many times. Remember the knee you scraped on the playground in fourth grade? No? Could it be because the scrape healed? Maybe your mother put Bactine on it and covered it with a bandage. Did that heal your knee? Or did you peek under the bandage and watch the wound go from red, angry-looking, and torn up the first day, to a dark reddish-brown hard scab a day later? Then the cut disappeared all together. That was your human body's self-healing mechanism in full swing.

You have also observed your body heal a number of bruises, cuts, colds, broken bones, and other injuries and illnesses, with or without medical intervention.

We all accepted as children that our bodies heal themselves. Why, then, don't we believe in those same self-healing powers as adults? Because we have been scared out of it by the medical profession. We are told that drugs or other expensive treatments are required to cure us. But how true is that assertion?

Most clinical trials for new drugs involve testing the effects of the trial medicine against a placebo, a dummy pill with no active ingredients, sometimes called a "sugar pill." The reports of these clinical trials disclose that some patients taking the sugar pill improve in the same way as those receiving the new drug. In fact, in some trials, the placebo did nearly as well as the drug itself at treating the condition at issue. How is this possible? Could it be that the patient's belief in the pill effected the improvement? If so, then the cure is attributable to manifesting, for we manifest what we truly believe.

But, you may say, there may have been some ingredient in the dummy pill that improved the patient's condition. Or the hope the clinical trial offered caused the improvement. Either way, it was something external to the patient that promoted the healing, you say, not manifesting. Point taken. Then consider the following scenarios:

*   *   *

Example A: When you were a toddler and hurt your elbow, what did you do? You went to mother, of course, and she kissed the boo-boo and told you she had made it "all better." The pain did in fact go away. Was it the kiss that stopped the pain?

Discussion: Some parents will say that all mom did was distract you from the pain, which was then forgotten. Distraction works because children have short attention spans. Sounds logical. But the nerve cells transmitting pain do not require the mind's attention to them in order to transmit their signals. The body feels pain whether or not we are conscious of it. People with chronically painful conditions often awaken from a sound sleep due to pain, although they were not thinking about pain in their sleep. Similarly, infants feel pain though their minds are not developed enough to think the word "pain."

While it is true that we experience less pain when distracted from dwelling on it, could it also be true that mom's kiss and reassurance created a *belief* that the pain was gone? And that *belief* manifested the reality of being pain-free? When you were a child you accepted this. Why did you stop?

＊　　　＊　　　＊

Example B: When as a child you were afraid of taking a math (or other) test, did you ever get a stomachache the morning of the test?

Discussion: Yes, you did. Certainly you know by now that you gave yourself the stomachache in an attempt to get out of taking the test. But your mother saw through it and sent you to school anyway. So now you know that you can make yourself sick if you try. If you believe that you can make the body ill, why not believe you can make it well?

＊　　　＊　　　＊

Example C: Have you heard stories of older married couples where one spouse dies within days to months of the other? We often say the survivor of the two then died of a broken heart. Is this the opposite of self-healing? Self-imposed death?

Discussion: The second spouse may very well have manifested a terminal condition in response to a *belief* that life is not worth living without his lifelong mate. If that sounds plausible to you, how is it that you believe you can manifest illness, and ultimately death, but cannot do the opposite?

✳   ✳   ✳

What is standing in the way of believing that our bodies can self-heal?

One powerful impediment is human animal laziness. Our bodies, like many other animals, prefer not to work for something if there is an easier way to get it. Pharmaceutical companies offer an easy way. Many of us would much rather take a pill to resolve physical discomfort than adopt healthier behaviors. How many times have we seen someone on cholesterol-lowering medication feasting on a diet of burgers and fries? Who wants to reduce stress when headaches can be treated with drugs? Why spend hours cooking nutritious meals when vitamins in a bottle are available? The miracle of modern medicine is that there is a pill for just about every symptom. So, many people rely on a one-second swallow rather than lifelong healthy habits to promote healing.

We may also have spiritual roadblocks to believing in self-healing. Some may argue that being unhappy or in pain is just our lot in life. We accept suffering as penance for sins or acts of omission. If Source intended that we suffer physical ailments as punishment, why design the human body with a built-in repair mechanism?

There are many, many reasons why we may have lost our childhood belief in our own healing powers. Donald M. Epstein, D.C., the founder of Network Chiropractic (an energy-based healing modality), has identified thirty-four such excuses in his wonderfully enlightening book *Healing Myths, Healing Magic*.[16] Some of them are bound to resonate with each of us.

We Light Being souls likewise have innate self-healing abilities. The soul repairs itself through resolution and healing of emotional issues created during physical lives. Just as it is imperative that the body repair itself to survive, it is crucial that a soul resolve the emotional problems being human creates, not only to evolve but also to live the joyous physical life Source intended. Why? Because when we have unresolved emotional problems, we unconsciously manifest physical reality from that state, thereby setting ourselves up to experience more of the same types of problems. This is partly why we seem to encounter the same bad situations over and over again.

How does human life create emotional problems for a soul?

We have all been taught through human example to "stuff" our feelings; we train ourselves not to react in various settings—no matter how we might feel—so as not to embarrass our parents, bosses, or loved ones. Through repetition over the years, that stuffing act becomes habit. Pretty soon we have shoved most of our emotional reactions right into our physical guts, and into our souls. Those buried emotions do not disappear. They fester. And they bleed into our unconscious motivations driving present day behavior. It is time to dig up those buried emotions, experience them (perhaps for the first time), heal them, and move on to happier lives.

Moving on seems to be an impossible task for some of us. We can thank our human hosts for that trait. Humans adapt quickly to just about any set of circumstances, even painful ones, and resist change. When those two human inclinations (adaptation and resistance to change) are triggered together, we can become stuck in a single behavior pattern or an entire way of life. People end up mired in self-destructive cycles in just this way. Then, because of the human adaptation response, those painful circumstances eventually feel normal. Once this new norm is accepted, our healing attempts seem strange and abnormal. Healing also signals "change" to the body, which it resists, leaving poor humans with very little motivation to return to health.

Becoming "set in our ways" defeats not only self-healing but also the very purpose of experiencing human life. As a supremely curious being, Source seeks new experiences for itself and us, not the same daily routine year after year. Once we have couch-potatoed our way through every rerun of *Law & Order*, watching TV ceases to be an evolutionary experience. After having spent a few years as an addict, we have fully consumed that way of life. No more is required to wrest nuances of experience out of overuse or abuse of a drug, gambling, food, or drink. It is time to move on to new adventures, as we heal our host bodies from the damage accumulated along the way.

Similarly, if we have spent many years trying to right a childhood wrong, or craving the love withheld by our parents, or desperately seeking the approval we sought at age eight, we most likely have garnered all the evolutionary experiences we can from those efforts. The most that can be done now is repeat the same behaviors and suffer the same results. It is time to move on to more fulfilling times in our lives.

We must make the effort to heal ourselves. We can change our lives only if we heal the pain and impediments that have scarred us as the result of emotional and physical traumas. Otherwise, our attention will be forever diverted to our wounds, with the intention to address them ever present in our souls. What happens when we give intense attention and intention to a thought? We manifest it into reality.

Manifesting from unhealed perspectives, of course, keeps us stuck in the same types of scenarios that created the emotional traumas in the first instance. We must heal the traumas, retrain our hosts to new behaviors, and give gratitude for what we have experienced—with the intention not to *repeat* it.

This process—experience, emotional reaction, and resolution of the emotion—is the cornerstone of our spiritual evolution. It is how we advance from one level of awareness to another. How? By changing our perspective. As we gain experiences, and *feel* how they impact us, we begin to understand that the pain we feel is a consequence of our own behavior choices. Though we may have started out blaming someone else, through introspection we come to realize that our actions played an equally important part in the unwanted outcome. We resolve not to repeat that behavior as we process the guilt of knowing that we "did it to ourselves." We then seek to understand why we would subject ourselves to such a painful experience. What drove us to act that way in the first place? As we begin to unravel our underlying motivations, the seed of forgiveness is planted. Eventually, "understanding begets compassion. And compassion is the heart of unconditional love, our path back to the Source."[17] It is through experiencing and healing our own emotional traumas that we gain the broader perspective needed to love unconditionally.

*   *   *

Question 2: Do you believe that as a Light Being soul you can heal your own emotional wounds so that they do not recur lifetime after lifetime?

Discussion: Once again, of course you do! Remember when your first boyfriend or girlfriend broke your heart? You thought the pain would never go away. You believed completely that you would never love again and would remember that heartbreak for the rest of your life. You wailed that your life was over. Do you remember that pain now? Do you even remember the boy or girl?

You healed yourself. You did. Self-healing is part of our innate spiritual nature.

A broken heart from a romantic misadventure is an obvious emotional trauma. What if the cause of our emotional pain is not so obvious? Our lives are so complicated and fast-paced we often do not have time to acknowledge our emotions, much less their causes. How, then, do we initiate emotional healing?

A powerful way of identifying and resolving emotional problems affecting body and soul is a technique called "Focusing ®." Focusing is the term coined by a group of psychologists at the University of Chicago, led by Eugene T. Gendlin, Ph.D., for a structured method of communicating directly with the body. The process relies upon the unspoken fact that we, as souls, can detach our awareness from that of the body to observe its emotional condition.

Through Focusing, we can ask the body simply and directly to tell us what is wrong by giving us a "felt sense" of it. Dr. Gendlin describes the body's wisdom as a collective "felt sense" rather than as thought:

> A felt sense is not a mental experience but a physical one. *Physical.* A bodily awareness of a situation or person or event. An internal aura that encompasses everything you feel and know about the given subject at a given time— encompasses it and communicates it to you all at once rather than detail by detail. . . .
>
> Let me illustrate. Think of two people who play a major role in your life. Any two people. I'll call them John and Helen in this discussion, but substitute the names of your own people.
>
> Let your mind slide back and forth between these two people. Notice the inner aura that seems to come into existence when you let your attention dwell on John, the sense of "all about John." Notice the entirely different aura of Helen.
>
> The inner aura as you think of each person isn't made up of discrete bits of data that you consciously add together in your mind. In thinking of Helen, you don't laboriously list all her physical and personal traits one by one. You don't think, "Oh yes, Helen: she's 5'6" tall, has blond hair and brown eyes and a small mole next to her ear, talks in a high voice, gets upset easily, wants to be a playwright, likes Chinese food, needs to lose weight ...." Nor do you list each detail of your relationship with her.
>
> There are undoubtedly millions of such bits of data that describe Helen as you know her, but these millions of bits aren't delivered to you one by one, as thoughts. Instead, they are given to you all at once, as *bodily felt.* The sense of "all about Helen"—including every one of those thousands of bits of data that you have seen, felt, lived, and stored over the years—comes to you all at once, as a single great aura sensed in your body.[18]

That felt sense is accessed and understood through the Six Focusing Movements, each described in greater detail in Dr. Gendlin's book *Focusing*. His brief summary of them is as follows:

1. Clear a space

   How are you? What's between you and feeling fine?

   Don't answer; let what comes in your body do the answering.

   Don't go into anything.

   Greet each concern that comes. Put each aside for a while, next to you.

   Except for that, are you fine?

2. Felt sense

   Pick one problem to focus on.

   Don't go into the problem. What do you sense in your body when you recall the whole of that problem?

   Sense all of that, the sense of the whole thing, the murky discomfort or the unclear body-sense of it.

3. Get a handle

   What is the quality of the felt sense?

   What one word, phrase, or image comes out of this felt sense?

   What quality-word would fit it best?

4. Resonate

   Go back and forth between word (or image) and the felt sense. Is that right?

   If they match, have the sensation of matching several times.

   If the felt sense changes, follow it with your attention.

   When you get a perfect match, the words (images) being just right for this feeling, let yourself feel that for a minute.

5. Ask

   "What is it, about the whole problem, that makes me

so _____?" . . .
What would it feel like if it was all OK?
Let the body answer:
What is in the way of that?
6. Receive
Welcome what came. Be glad it spoke.

It is only one step on this problem, not the last.
Now that you know where it is, you can leave it and
come back to it later.
Protect it from critical voices that interrupt.[19]

The felt sense may well be an emotional response of which we were previously unaware. It had been stuffed down deep inside precisely so we would not feel it. But the body felt the stuffed emotion physically. And that emotion is crying out to be heard in the only way it can—by causing physical discomfort. Using Focusing, we can discover not only the location of the stuffed emotion but also its nature and origin. Once we understand the emotion and its origin, we can let it go by changing our perspective on the events giving rise to it. We can resolve the emotional response we have avoided and heal the related physical problems.

The beauty of Focusing is that through it we can experience two simultaneous levels of awareness. We do it by following the six-step process described above. When we take the observer or questioner's position, asking the body what it feels, we have separated our awareness from that of the human being we inhabit. The human's awareness is focused on the physical sensations. We observer-souls are attempting to find a word that fits the body's discomfort. An insight that describes and explains the body's pain or concern appears. We are aware of the body's sensation at the same time we are receiving insight into its meaning—two levels of awareness.

During one of my own Focusing sessions, conducted by a trained facilitator, I experienced and voiced out loud insights from the three levels of awareness of human, soul, and Light Being. The purpose of the Focusing was to relieve post-traumatic stress symptoms that started after an automobile accident. After asking the body what its emotional state was just before actual impact, the facilitator and I heard my voice say, "I don't want to go. I'll be hit." The facilitator asked what I wanted to do about that situation. My response referred to myself as soul in the third person, "She [soul] wants to trust the girl [not to make an illegal turn]." Clearly the "she" in this context was not the body, as its words, spoken first, proved my body was clutched by fear. Then I spoke out again unexpectedly, saying, "She [the soul] gets that from me. I know that every experience will further growth and evolution." That last voice was I—the Being of Light I truly am. Fearless. Wanting only to experience human life for Source.

Through Focusing, I was able to gently unwind the fight-flight-freeze reaction that still gripped my body two years after the accident because of its inability to do anything to avoid the collusion. I also resolved and healed the anger I felt toward the teenager who hit me. And, because my Light Being understanding was voiced and accepted, I experienced healing from all three levels. Focusing might work this way for you too.

Self-healing can, and should, take place simultaneously on all three levels: the human body level, the soul level, and the level of awareness we enjoy in our Light Being state.

Human Perspective	Light Being Perspective	Source's Perspective
Stem cells repair damage to my body.	Resolution of human-created emotional issues repairs trauma to my "soul" personality.	I heal the damage perceived by one of my manifestations by changing the parameters of the manifestation itself.

Physical illness and injury can be healed by allowing the body's own repair mechanisms to work through their cellular processes. Traditional medical treatments can assist healing, as will energy therapies like Reiki or Healing Touch, and many of the holistic therapies available today. A combination of modalities may be most beneficial.

There are many techniques for healing emotional traumas to the soul: introspection, psychotherapy, talking things over with a trusted friend, getting a different perspective on the situation from someone whose views we respect, and accessing Universal Knowledge. We may have to sample several methods to find one or more that allow us to release our emotional burdens.

More sophisticated self-healing, of course, takes place at the Light Being level. To understand how, we must reexamine how we came to be here as souls.

As extensions of Source's self-awareness, we Light Beings can separate part of our own consciousness—one level of our multiple simultaneous layers of awareness—and reduce its Energy so that it can harmonize with physical manifestations like Earth and its inhabitants. That "soul" Energy enters into a human to live its life as intimate companion.

Part of our own Light Being consciousness thus enters into the physical manifestation of Earth, much like Neo would sojourn into the Matrix in the movie of that name. And, just as Neo learned to manipulate the Matrix—jumping off tall buildings without falling, dodging bullets—by changing his beliefs about the Matrix, we can learn to subtly change the manifestation we perceive as human reality by adopting new beliefs about it. We can deliberately rewrite the content of our own physical reality, and thus our experience of it, through a spiritual mechanism similar to lucid dreaming.

Lucid dreaming is the phenomenon of consciously observing a dream in progress as the witnessing presence, and then knowingly changing the dream's direction. Lucid dreaming occurs when we souls become aware of dreams, take the observer position in them, and then interject something into the content (similar to day-dreaming). The purpose might be to ask what a particular dream sequence means, or to plant an idea similar to a post-hypnotic suggestion. Lucid dreaming can be learned through practice.

At our Light Being level of awareness, we can consciously revise what we believe about our physical existence, similar to how a lucid dreamer alters a dream. Human life is a manifestation co-created by Source and those Light Beings (including us) with an interest in Earth as a physical environment. We can individually modify those portions of our human experience that we alone manifest. We can change what we believe about our physical condition at the Light Being level. Rewrite the scene. Manifest differently.

If having physical or emotional pain is not the primary purpose for selecting our human hosts, we can improve our well being by resetting the parameters of the "health" portion of our human manifestation to eliminate certain symptoms. Of course, the level of focused attention and intention needed to do this is extremely high. Still, it is an innate skill we all possess as Beings of Light that can be accessed by raising our awareness level.

Undoubtedly this concept of Light Beings rewriting the scripts of our lives sounds very foreign. Yet, we are all intimately familiar with the phenomenon in another context. We call it prayer. Ultimately, all healing takes place at the level of Source's manifestation of the universe and all it contains. We know that intuitively. We have all sought a revision in the manifestation we call our human life by asking Source to heal us. Because we are one with Source, prayer constitutes a form of self-healing as well.

10

✳ Stop Judging

WE ARE IN THE habit of judging all the time. We compare new people, places, and things to our past experiences and comfort zone parameters. Today is nicer than yesterday. My feet do not hurt like they did last week. That dog is barking more than usual. Judging has become so ingrained in our thinking that we are completely unaware of it most of the time. But we should become aware of judging.

As explained in more detail in Chapter 15 of *BACKWARDS: Returning to Our Source for Answers*, forming judgments about people, places, and things is a human character trait. Light Beings are not judgmental. We souls adopt this human character trait by osmosis, unless we make a conscious effort to remain true to our spiritual nature and stop judging.

The admonition to stop judging does not mean we should stop analyzing, assessing, or evaluating data to make informed choices. Nor do we have to relinquish personal preferences. Rather, we could stop condemning or devaluing another person, place, or thing for failure to conform to our own expectations. And, we can stop limiting our perspectives by comparing everything to the human herd's "norm."

Part of becoming enlightened, becoming more aware of who we really are, involves noticing all the times we form judgments. More than that, we can analyze how those judgments have affected our ability to love unconditionally.

The following questions and examples are designed to make you more aware of judgments that may have seeped into your soul personality and/or thought patterns, and which now prevent you from enjoying all the love you have to offer.

Question 1: Below are photographs of two famous people who have done remarkable things from the human perspective. You are at a party where you know no one. So it is up to you to approach someone to strike up a conversation. Which of these two gentlemen would you choose to get to know?

Discussion: Steven Hawking, pictured[20] on the right, is a Nobel Prize winning physicist. Ted Bundy, pictured[21] on the left, is the notorious serial killer.

Human perspective. Did you follow the stereotypes prevalent in human culture and assume the physically attractive man to be the better choice of party companion? Judging based on physical attractiveness alone might have led you to your death at the hands of the charming, but deadly, Mr. Bundy. Do you still want to make your choices based on human judgment?

No matter how valid we believe our opinions are, forming a snap judgment about another person can be dangerous and erroneous—as this exercise shows. This is particularly true if our opinion is based solely on pre-conceived notions, rather than honest interaction.

Light Being perspective. At our Light Being level of awareness we *know* that physical appearance merely masks the glorious spark of Source self-awareness inside. We are all Source. We are all worthy of friendship and unconditional love. Even the serial killer. Even someone whose physical appearance repulses us. A soul awakened to its true nature knows that it cannot possibly have sufficient information or perspective to accurately judge anything while in human form. Such a soul tries to accept life just as it unfolds, without judgment.

*   *   *

Question 2: Assume your five-year old child comes to you with a fantastic story of getting out of his body and flying around the neighborhood. He delighted in watching his little friends bulldozing new highways with Bob the Builder yellow plastic trucks in the sandbox at the end of the street. Your son asks why his buddies would not talk to him while he was flying around. What is your response?

    A. "Oh, honey, you were just dreaming that. Your friends would have talked to you if it had been real."

    B. "Oh, you kidder. You have such a vivid imagination."

    C. You recognize that your child has displayed normal Light Being talents and support the experience by giving him reassurance and information about what happened.

    D. You fear your child has had a dissociative reaction and call a therapist.

Discussion: Small children have an easier time displaying skills and abilities innate to their Light Being nature because they feel it is natural. Parents and teachers are the ones who treat soul talents as unnatural, implying they should be avoided or hidden. As a parent you have a difficult choice in this situation. Do you encourage development of the tender soul's full range of talents or just the animal ones? The former choice will be more beneficial for evolution but will likely create opportunities for the child to be ridiculed by society. The latter deprives the soul of enlightenment but protects the child from emotional trauma.

Choices A, B and D reflect human judgment based on fear of being outside the human herd's, and one's own personal, comfort zones. The initial impulse is to label the experience as abnormal and attempt to prevent a recurrence by stigmatizing either the experience, or the boy's interpretation of it.

A. *Dreaming* and B. *Imagination.* Calling an out-of-body episode a dream may well confuse your son because he knows he was not asleep. He might even lose some trust in your guidance because what you are saying conflicts with his own personal experience. Your son trusts his own eyes. Other consequences of choice A or B may be: (1) your child loses respect for, and trust in, his own observations and judgments, for surely Mom would not lie to him about what he experienced; or (2) your boy still believes he was out-of-body and so begins to fear he is "weird" and unacceptable, and therefore unlovable. He resolves never to tell you events like this again. You have lost the opportunity to share your son's spiritual life.

C. *Normal soul behavior.* Obviously, you have to know out-of-body travel is normal spiritual behavior in order to recognize it as such in your child. If you are not familiar with out-of-body experiences, there is a wealth of reading material available. After familiarizing yourself with the subject, tell your son that he is a soul, a spiritual being, who lives inside his human body. One of his powers as a soul is the ability to get out-of-body and travel around in spirit form. Because his spirit is invisible, his friends did not see him. That is why they did not talk to him. If you think this is too much information, you can at least tell your son that what happened is normal, and that everyone can do it, though most people do not remember how. Assure your son that his experience was valid and you appreciate his sharing it with you.

D. *Dissociative reaction.* If choice D is your reaction, your child will sense your fear and immediately become afraid himself, unless you completely restore his confidence. Calling a therapist will not be comforting.

I learned from Universal Knowledge while I was dead that humans have a complete misunderstanding about mental illness. Many of the behaviors we call illness are actually normal for the soul. The reason we mischaracterize some behavior as illness is simply because it is so far outside the herd norms. It is society's judgment that makes it an illness—not the person's behavior.

Out-of-body travel is normal for the soul. It is not a mental illness of the body. If you label it as mental illness, and treat your child as though he were ill, you will create a far more damaging condition for him than out-of-body travel. He will come to think of himself as crazy and unlovable. That impression will destroy his self-esteem and stigmatize him not only in this life but possibly into succeeding ones as well.

*   *   *

Question 3: Do you believe you make valid judgments about people from observing their behavior?

Discussion: Of course, you do! We all believe our opinions are valid, or we would not have formed them in the first place. What might escape our awareness, however, is the fact that our judgments are based on the data we have garnered from one limited perspective. In other words, we might think differently if we could view the situation from the vantage points of the other participants.

Example A. I once had an employee whom I fired after working less than a month. Sally thought she had been unjustly terminated for missing work to repeat a weekend self-improvement seminar. I had approved traveling time off the first time Sally attended the seminar, so she assumed I would do so again. I told Sally that she was free to make her own choice about the seminar; but she would not have a job waiting for her if she missed any more work.

My other employees also thought I had unjustly fired Sally for attending the seminar. In fact, I terminated her employment because she had failed to work eleven of the twenty-one days of her short employment history. My other employees were unaware of Sally's other absences. Each employee in this example believed her opinion to be the valid one, based upon the facts she saw. I wonder whether my employees' opinions would have changed had they been in the employer's position.

Example B. Alice is playing hostess to an overnight guest tomorrow night. Mary is her neighbor. Mary thinks Alice should clean her house, go grocery shopping, and schedule a dinner party to entertain her guest. Alice has done none of these things. Mary offers to help Alice make the preparations that Mary thinks should be made. Alice says her guest will be fine. Mary is losing her mind over Alice's lack of social graces.

Mary's opinion of what should be done to prepare for a houseguest is based upon her upbringing in a socially sophisticated Southern family. Alice, who is artistic and rarely follows societal norms, holds the opinion that her relationship with her houseguest is more important than material things. So she rebuffs Mary's offer of help with cleaning, shopping, and cooking.

Mary, whose motives are good and pure in that she really does want to help, does not realize that she is actually judging Alice's lifestyle based upon social norms that are important only to Mary. Anything that meets social conventions is good in Mary's mind. Behavior that falls outside social norms is bad. Mary is unable to see that her viewpoint is completely animal in nature because it values conformity to herd behavior patterns.

Alice's values, on the other hand, are more in line with our Light Being nature. At the spiritual level, material goods have no value whatsoever. What matters is whether we treat each other with unconditional love. Alice has chosen to honor her relationship with her houseguest in ways unfamiliar to Mary.

*　　*　　*

Question 4: Do you believe the deity will judge your life after you die?

Discussion: Religious writers have assumed our gods must be judgmental because humans are. Many faiths embrace a deity who watches everything we do, and who judges us unworthy of a joyous afterlife if we fail to walk the straight and narrow path of righteousness. The Source I met in the afterlife was nothing like that. Nothing at all.

I was not judged at any time during my afterlife transition— from leaving the human body to merging into Source's Energy field. The only semblance of judgment was the life review, where I was the only one reviewing my human behavior from the Light Being perspective of unconditional love. Even then, my own judgment had no eternal consequences like the punishment many people fear.

Human fear of judgment and condemnation is thus unfounded, based on what I experienced and what I learned of Universal Knowledge on this subject.

The three levels of perspective on judgment can be summarized as shown in the following chart:

Human Perspective	Light Being Perspective	Source's Perspective
I will be judged at death for my sins and punished accordingly.	My "soul" level of awareness will re-experience its human behavior, and all its consequences, during the life review. It will review its actions from the perspective of whether they reflected unconditional love.	I do not judge the actions of my manifestations.

The closest analogy to behavior supervisors I have ever encountered are the Light Being "councils" whose function is to assist a soul in meeting its own goals. Councils do not tell us what to do. Nor do they set rules for soul behavior. My own council is a group of Light Beings who care deeply about my evolution and well being, and, who, because they remain at much higher levels of awareness, can observe my behavior unclouded by human personality. They have the universal perspective I lack while here, and can advise me when I am not doing what I planned for this life.

Many near-death survivors make dramatic changes in their lifestyles. I did not—at least not immediately. Consequently, my council called me back to the Light within weeks after my initial beyond death experience. On this occasion, while my body slept, I returned to the Light to meet with a group of Light Beings with oversight roles. Several brilliant Beings unknown to me seemed to be gathered in a type of formal conclave, similar to a legal hearing or tribunal, with my human life the focus of attention. It was evident to me that each person in the group had a keen interest in how well I was doing back in human life, and that they were not entirely satisfied. All I can remember now is that the council felt I was not pursuing what I had planned during my beyond death experience. So, they were there to guide and support me in my mission. I do not remember exactly what they expected me to do, but my conscious mind later interpreted my instructions to be to start pursuing my new spiritual mission.

A second meeting with my council seven years later was more dramatic and traumatic, probably because I was very ill. I was admitted to the hospital through the emergency room shortly after this event for conditions that still affect me seven years later.

Once again, while the body slept, I drifted to another level of consciousness to what appeared to be a hastily called gathering in the Light. The manifested Earth-like setting appeared more like a conference room than a formal hearing chamber. The members were settling into chairs around a crowded table when I arrived. Three council members joined the group after I did, confirming my impression of spontaneity.

Two of the last three Beings to enter displayed the faces of my parents for just a second before that illusion was replaced with their luminescent Light Being forms. My parents' participation both thrilled and shocked me. Their human hosts had died years before this council meeting, so I was excited to see their faces again even for a moment. I felt my parents had given me the wonderful gift of recognition to reassure me in advance of the meeting about to take place. The fact that my human parents were on my council disturbed me, however, as I felt I had not respected their guidance as well as I should have while they were in the body. (I might have taken them more seriously had I known they were evolved enough to be on my council!)

The last council member to arrive appeared in human form, projected a sense of rush, and remained in human appearance for some time. When I raised my gaze to his, he looked me straight in the eye and mouthed the word "surprise!" And I was surprised! I recognized this Being as a human I know this life as Jeff, though I cannot recall now *which* Jeff. An alarm went off in my mind seeing someone from my human life, as if some emergency had triggered a recall of even undercover agents.

This second council meeting was brief and to the point. The Energy Beings told me that extremely difficult times lay ahead— times that would cause me grave suffering. The council acknowledged my body's illness and weakened condition, intimating my human might not have sufficient strength to recover. The council gave me the option of staying in human life, or reawakening to Energy Being level right then to avoid the suffering.

They made it clear that if I chose to leave human life, it would not be considered a breach of contract on my part. (I had assigned myself the goal of telling people what I experienced in the afterlife after I returned to the body. That was the contract they were relieving me from performing.) If I stayed in my human host, they said, I must endure constant suffering. Despite what they showed me about my future, I chose to stay in human form. My motivation at the time was that I did not want to miss witnessing what is going to happen in Earth's future.

When I awoke immediately after making the decision, I was certain the meeting had taken place. Yet the amnesia of human nature has robbed me of the memory of whether the choice I had made was between enduring the illness and recovery from it, or, living through the most severe part of the transition in epochs. All I know for certain is that my choice was whether or not to "go through with it." The "it" part is now unclear.

It is easy to see how others who have experienced similar council meetings might interpret them as evidence of judgment after death. But the evolved Light Beings who volunteer to be on councils exude concern, not judgment. They vibrate at very high frequencies, very close to the Source's, and reflect its unconditional love. Their function is to serve the needs of Energy Beings souls who have chosen to experience human life, by offering us an objective outside observer's perspective at times when it is crucially needed.

*　　*　　*

While being judgmental may be an innate part of the human experience, it is a character trait we would do well to try to conquer. Our judgments are almost always in error because our points of reference are so limited by these physical bodies. More importantly, judging others robs us of the opportunity to enjoy unconditional love. We can only give each other unconditional love by accepting one another just as we are, instead of judging each other's faults and foibles.

11

* Treat Each Other Responsibly

How MANY TIMES DID your parents try to teach you, "Sticks and stones may break my bones, but words will never hurt me?" Did you believe it as a child? Do you believe it now? We all know that words can and do hurt us. Some words are intrinsically hurtful and consistently arouse hurt feelings in most of us.

Both humans and Light Being souls have emotions, sometimes supersensitive ones, as part of their innate natures created by Source. We ignore that fact at our peril.

Proponents of some spirituality-based life plans defy common knowledge when they assert that emotions are merely thoughts leaping into action, and we can therefore consciously decide how we will feel about something. Teachers of these plans claim we can improve our lives, and raise our level of consciousness, by learning to control our emotions. This logic flies in the face of our shared experience that emotions emerge spontaneously. The truth is, emotions arise automatically in both humans and Light Beings, in response to stimuli. Very little, if any, thought precedes them.

The viewpoint that being emotionless is a higher state of consciousness reflects lack of knowledge of the fact that we continue to have emotions after the human body dies. If feelings and emotions are simple thoughts we should learn to master to be more evolved, then why do we continue to experience emotions in the much more highly evolved state of awareness we call the afterlife? Indeed, the highest state of consciousness in our universe—Source itself—is an emotional entity.

Because feelings and emotions are valid, innate aspects of our dual natures, we should not learn to control them but rather to understand them. Feel them. Express them. Hear the messages feelings are trying to relate. We should honor the fact that everyone else has real emotions, valid feelings. And, we should strive to treat each other's feelings with consideration in our daily interactions.

Emotions do not cause interpersonal relationship problems. Behaviors do. Whether, and how, we choose to act on our emotions may create conflict. Some behavior choices hurt others. Our behavior, then, is what we need to control—not our emotions. Our behavior patterns can be consciously changed, through effort, once we understand and resolve the emotions spawning them.

We cannot hope to become more evolved, much less unconditionally loving, if we choose to ignore the emotional content of our interactions. In fact, we are responsible to a degree for the emotions we deliberately arouse in others, as we will see and *feel* during our life reviews in the Light.

Here are a few situations from my own life, before my personal encounter with Source, that illustrate how important it is to recognize, and take into account, each other's emotions before acting:

*   *   *

Example A: I am generally willing to accept that I may be wrong about most anything. But, one of my many failings is that I overreact when non-lawyers argue that they know more than I do about an area of law I know well.

For example, many years ago my best friend "Alice" attended a seminar on sexual harassment conducted by her employer's Human Resources Department. That weekend Alice and I went to a movie. She told me about the seminar and mentioned she had learned that a certain behavior constituted sexual harassment. Thinking I was sharing an important point, I replied that the federal appeals court for our jurisdiction had just recently ruled that behavior *not* to be sexual harassment. Alice proceeded to argue how wrong I was, and how her HR VP knew what he was talking about, while I worked up a really big head of steam. I tried calmly to explain that the law could be different in different jurisdictions. Finally exasperated, I heard myself saying to her:

Why is it that you always have to know more about everything than I do? Why can't you just this once acknowledge that, as an attorney with fifteen years experience advising clients about employment law and litigating sexual harassment cases, I might possibly know more than your HR guy does about sexual harassment, which is, after all, a legal concept?

You can imagine how that went over.

How could we have treated each other responsibly, and with kindness, in this conversation?

Discussion: A possible Light Being viewpoint is: Nanci, you were letting your human ego get in the way of recognizing Alice's distress. It was obvious that she had an unexpected emotional response. You should have let Alice have her say, backed off, and dealt privately with your own issue of competitiveness reflected in what you said to Alice.

A human perspective might be: Alice should have given you credit for something that is clearly within your expertise and just accepted what you said. (Not surprisingly, I preferred this view at the time of the argument.)

A good compromise might have been for Alice to have heard me out, but to respond that for purposes of working with her company's HR Department she would have to follow what she had been taught.

All of these perspectives, each with its own wisdom and appeal, miss the point. The crux of the interaction was not who was right about what constitutes sexual harassment. The significance of the story is the picture it paints of relationship conflict and how *not* to handle it.

Alice and I focused solely on what we were *doing* at the time of the argument, not what we were *being* in the relationship. We were *being* human. We identified with our bodies' employment roles, took opposing positions, and squared off like two bulls about to charge each other, horns first. We acted like animals—human animals. And it was human emotion that caused the conflict, i.e., a competitive battle to be the one who was right.

Alice had simply told me about her week, including the sexual harassment seminar she knew I would find interesting. She had not been trying to play legal expert. Judging from her reaction, Alice must have taken my comment as an attempt to make *her* wrong, to assert my own superiority as Alpha dog legal beagle in what had always been a relationship between equals. She retaliated by "pushing my buttons" on what she knew to be a volatile issue.

I felt Alice had unfairly attacked me out of the blue. I was trying to be helpful by providing free legal advice. It seemed logical to me that, since Alice knew I litigated sexual harassment cases, she would listen unemotionally to what I had to say and then move on to the next topic. I did not say, or imply, that *Alice* was wrong. Nor did I intend to compete with her or assert any superiority—at least not until I got angry with her arguing that *I* was wrong, at which point I proceeded to throw my superior knowledge in Alice's face.

Neither Alice nor I set out to do harm. But what we each said was known by us to be hurtful to us. Had we taken responsibility for knowing each other as well as we did, we could have recognized in advance that we had battled through this issue before and had both been left bleeding. We could then have made different word choices to avoid the argument.

I knew Alice did not respond well when I went into lawyer mode. I also knew she could not tolerate being corrected. Yet, knowing this, I put my own emotional need to be recognized as the expert above what I knew about my friend's sensitivities. I should have kept the legal update to myself.

Alice likewise took no responsibility for knowing me well. She knew from previous conversations like this one that telling me I was wrong about the law would light me up like napalm. She could have chosen to ignore my legal advice and gone on with recounting her day.

How could we have turned the situation into one that enriched us both? By being aware in the moment of our own emotional issues, by respecting each other's emotions, and by taking responsibility for the predictable consequences of our own actions.

I was partly responsible for Alice's hurt feelings because I knew before I told her about the new sexual harassment ruling that she might feel I was correcting her, which she always took to be criticism. I could have been present in the moment enough to be aware that Alice was sharing her life with me, not inviting a legal debate. After she told me I was wrong, and before I escalated the argument, I could have remembered I get hot when non-lawyers challenge my legal opinions, and it always turns out badly when I argue the point. No one deserves being subjected to an argument with a trial lawyer, if they are not getting paid for it.

Alice was partly responsible for my hurt feelings. She knew from experience how I would react to her saying my legal opinion was wrong. Alice could have been present in the moment enough to realize I was trying to help her in her job by sharing what I thought was information important for her to know. And, she could have trusted that I would never intentionally put her down because I had never done so before.

We could have honored each other by agreeing that we did not care about sexual harassment, but did care about each other, and said, "let's just drop it" after the initial exchange. We could have recognized the power struggle for what it was—we were fighting for dominance, a goal that has no place at all in a friendship.

We would have honored each other, and ourselves, had we been able to open up emotionally and discuss our underlying feelings, instead of spewing accusations. Such a conversation might have been a growth experience, as well as one that bonded us closer together.

＊　＊　＊

Example B: What if the emotional stakes had been higher than in the last exercise? Should the analysis be the same?

Alice and I had the same argument later, at a time when she was taking hormone shots in an attempt to get pregnant through in-vitro fertilization. I was waiting to hear whether the appearance of new calcium deposits in my post-surgery mammograms meant I had breast cancer. We were both emotional powder kegs.

Alice and her husband had consulted an attorney about adoption as a plan B. The attorney told them they would not be allowed to adopt an infant because they were over forty. I, naturally, felt the need to correct that statement, ostensibly to relieve my friend's misery over the prospect of never having a child. I told Alice that no law prevented couples over forty from adopting; the problem was that the Probate Court Judge had a personal prejudice against older couples. I told her I thought the Judge's ruling could be reversed on appeal if they wanted to try adoption.

Once again, Alice told me her attorney was right and I was wrong. Once again, I asked why she had to challenge my legal opinions, inasmuch as we had always readily accepted each other's opinions on every other subject.

Does the same analysis from the last example apply when the facts are so different? Does it make a difference that Alice was unable to control her emotions because of the physical effect of the hormone shots? Was the fact that my anxiety was running high an excuse for my behavior?

Discussion: The same analysis applies. Our respective heightened emotions called for heightened consideration by, and for, each other. The Light Being way of handling the situation would have been to acknowledge each other's state of distress, and to honor each other by dropping the issue and/or focusing on sharing our feelings. The power of being present in the moment, and stepping back from the body's torment to gain perspective, would have salvaged this encounter.

*　　*　　*

Example C: Assume an outwardly kind and loving woman, named Mary, has dedicated her life to running a charitable organization. She has chaired the Board of Directors for twenty years. Mary has counseled many, many hurting people who have sought services from the charity. She considers this role to be her mission from God.

Assume two new directors were appointed to the Board. Over time, the new directors began to talk about ways the charity's benefits could be made available to more people. The new directors convinced the Board it was a good idea to advertise and extend the charity's service area. Mary felt the new directors were challenging her leadership by implying she had not done enough. She was hurt. A subtle power struggle ensued, which Mary handled by going behind the scenes and convincing the other Directors to vote the new directors off the Board. Was Mary treating all parties responsibly and with respect?

Discussion: We do not know Mary's true motivations for getting the new directors voted off the Board.

If Mary's overriding concern was to eliminate conflict on an otherwise harmonious Board of Directors, that intent could have been a loving motivation. But there might have been ways of eliminating conflict during meetings without kicking directors off the Board. Mary's actions actually contributed to the conflict. And, she acted from animal instincts, not love. Mary exerted her power over the Board in an animal exhibition of dominance, driving off competing potential leaders.

Perhaps Mary's goal was to keep the charity small to reduce the risk that her position of power would be challenged. Mary may have derived significant satisfaction from her role as Board Chair, and a tremendous ego boost. If those were Mary's motivations in excluding the new directors, her actions were once again human-based. They arose from animal competitiveness and self-interest.

If Mary's actions were motivated by a desire to preserve the status quo, the old and familiar, that would also be acting from the human animal level of awareness. Fear of change is purely human. Light Being nature is to expand and grow. We Light Beings welcome new ideas, not shrink from them. Our natural curiosity compels us to try new things even when the old ways are perfectly fine.

Engaging in a power struggle in an attempt to preserve control is likewise human nature. It is an aspect of the animal tendency toward domination. Our spiritual nature is to recognize that we are all equal within Source. We each have our own purposes to serve and experiences to gain. The new Directors' idea of giving services to more people is an aspect of unconditional love.

Regardless of the reason, excluding the new directors from the Board for espousing new ideas does not appear to have been an act of unconditional love toward them. Allowing them to continue on the Board only if they conformed to the old group dynamics exemplifies *conditional* love.

Sometimes the most loving, giving people among us get stuck in human nature. We all do it from time to time. This exercise raises the question of how often our own attempts to give to others in a group setting, such as by working for a charity, disguises what are ultimately competitive or self-laudatory motives.

✳   ✳   ✳

Humans have inborn emotional reactions, just as they have innate instincts. All sentient animals do. Take, for example, your pet dog or cat. If every day for months you allowed your pet to jump up on the couch to join you sitting there, he would come to believe he is entitled to be on the couch. Then, if you suddenly one day pushed him off the couch, the dog or cat would be confused. The pet would also have an instant emotional reaction of feeling rejected—because the pet has been rejected. Depriving an animal of an entitlement that you established is a rejection and intrinsically hurtful. You trained your animal one way and then suddenly changed the rules on him. That feels like a betrayal.

Human animals respond the very same way. There are some actions and words that are intrinsically hurtful to the human personality. And no amount of therapy, insight, or trying to control one's emotions will ever change that. At least not until the human species evolves beyond its current state of emotional development.

Similarly, Light Being souls have inborn automatic emotional responses. Many emotional triggers have developed over a number of human lifetimes because repetitive human experiences have embedded traumas in the eternal personality of the soul. But, unlike our human hosts, we souls are capable of maturing in our emotional lives. Our ability to move from one level of awareness to another allows us to step back to gain a broader perspective on events. That more global vantage point helps to dilute the event's emotional content. We can also access the unconditional love of our Energy still in the Light to defuse emotional triggers.

The following chart summarizes how humans view their responsibility toward others, as well as the higher levels of awareness to which we can aspire:

Human Perspective	Light Being Perspective	Source's Perspective
I am not responsible for arousing someone else's emotions. They are.	I am responsible for how I make others feel and will relive their emotions during my life review.	We are all One, so ultimately all emotions are mine.

Because resolution of physical and emotional traumas is essential to spiritual evolution, we should use our spiritual tools to increase our ability to value others' emotions as we do our own. For our life reviews will cast us in the roles of everyone with whom we have ever interacted, and we will live all of their emotional responses to our behaviors. We can make that more pleasant by how we treat others now.

The weightiest reason for taking responsibility for how we treat others, for the emotional responses we engender in others, is the fact that all of our experiences merge into and become part of Source once we have completed our evolution through the manifested universe.

As discussed previously, everything in our universe is a manifestation projected within the mind of our Source. Source created the multitude of persons, places, and things in order to explore its own incredibly complex emotions. Source configured interrelationships and interactions capable of generating a wealth of feelings. So, while the physical world is manifested, and the events occurring here are not real, the emotional responses to those physical world events are very real. They are Source's own emotional reactions and should be respected as such.

12

✳ Manifest Consciously

Star light, star bright,
first star I see tonight,
I wish I may, I wish I might,
have this wish I wish tonight.

Do you remember whispering this to the heavens as a child? Childhood is full of fantasies and superstitions. If we make a wish while blowing out all the candles on our birthday cake, our wish will come true. Throwing a coin into a fountain as we wish makes the wish come true.

Wishing does not appear to be limited to childhood.

Some writers claim to have discovered an ancient law that governs whether our adult wishes come true. They say all we have to do to have all the material goods we want, and the life of our dreams, is think about it. The law of attraction will then draw to us all that we desire. The law of attraction is described as something comparable to the law of gravity. Gravity, as we know, is a scientific principle. Gravity can be measured and quantified through physics. It can be proven mathematically. So, by saying the law of attraction is like the law of gravity, those writers are giving their idea a scientific connotation when, in fact, there is no science behind it.

The so-called law of attraction is part of a much larger *spiritual* phenomenon I call "manifesting." Some writers and motivational speakers have based their entire message on one little piece of manifesting, probably because that piece is easily understood from the human perspective. The problem with the human viewpoint, however, is that it often brings us to a false conclusion.

For example, the most brilliant scholars in ancient Europe understood the world to be a flat plate, with the sun circling around it, because they saw the sun rising in the east every morning and setting in the west every evening. They could see from one horizon to the other and positively identify the Earth as flat. Many, many generations of human beings sincerely feared sailing past the tip of Spain because they would fall off the Earth. Christopher Columbus, of course, proved the Earth to be round. But until he did that, the Earth was flat as a matter of science. This is the limited perspective a human has.

Since Columbus' time, we have sent humans into space to observe our planet. We have all seen pictures of the Earth taken from outer space that prove it is round. Our global perspective has changed because science and technology have provided us with larger and broader vantage points. Does that make the ancient scholars wrong? No, they were correct—for their level of perspective, their level of evolution, and their place in time. Do we consider them right today? No, because we have a broader perspective.

To truly understand our Light Being ability to manifest physical reality, we must expand our perspective far beyond the confines of what is being called the law of attraction. And we must recognize manifesting for what it is—a spiritual power—not a scientific law governing the physical world.

✳ ✳ ✳

Question 1: Do you believe we can just think about something and create it in physical reality? Or is the deity the only one who can create reality?

Discussion: The Book *The Secret*[22] proclaims that if we think about something long enough, truly concentrate on it with intense desire, it will eventually appear in our lives. Earlier books on creating wealth had also concluded that thinking something literally makes it true—creates reality. That is only partly true. Some of our thoughts do create physical reality via the mechanism of manifesting. We do in fact create our own physical, emotional, and spiritual realities—to a point. And, of course, Source is ultimately responsible for all the manifestations we experience.

Books like *The Secret* go astray when they say that all we have to do is think about something with emotion and the *universe* will give it to us. These books tell us to look to something outside ourselves to fulfill wishes. Their authors do not clarify whether they mean the actual physical universe of stars, planets, and empty space will grant our wishes; or they are using "universe" as a euphemism for God or Source. They do, however, imply that manifesting comes from something external to us. Wishing for something is like ordering it from the catalog of the universe, says *The Secret*.[23]

Manifesting is not external to us. *We* manifest reality. *Source* manifests reality. Not the stars. Not coins in a fountain. Not the physical universe, which is itself a manifestation.

Human Perspective	Light Being Perspective	Source's Perspective
The universe grants my wishes.	I focus my attention and intention to manifest physical reality.	All of life transpires in my mind and is of my creation.

Manifesting is one of Source's innate abilities. Source's creative powers are such that it can conceive of an idea and project it as a visual thought within its own mind. Source then creatively crafts the details from its imagination. Artists do the same thing. The only difference between Source's artwork and that of a human artist is the medium used. Source constructs physical matter—it projects its own Energy outward in patterns that appear to humans to be solid matter—from pure thought. The artist uses that physical matter to construct representations of his/her thoughts.

We Light Beings likewise can construct physical matter reality with our own thoughts, because we are extensions of Source with the same innate abilities. We create physical matter by consciously focusing our "attention and intention" on manifesting a visual representation of what we imagine. We can manipulate Source Energy into patterns that human senses interpret to be Earth-like matter.

Why do humans think Source Energy patterns are solid matter? Because human beings have fairly poor sensory reception.

The first movie producers took photographs of actors in scenes every few seconds and strung them together to create a "moving picture." Projecting sequential frames of stills created movement to the human eye because the brain fills in the missing scenes to create harmony and continuity. Animations, or cartoons, were made the same way. Magic tricks utilize the same defects in human vision to fool the eye into believing the illusion. "The hand is faster than the eye" slogan captures this principle. Human eyes miss a lot, especially things moving at very fast speeds. Manifestations appear to be solid matter and real for the same reasons that moving pictures and magic tricks fool humans into accepting illusion as reality.

Manifesting convinces humans for the additional reason that

the brain tends to create patterns out of chaos. The TV show *Numbers* demonstrated this when the character Professor Charlie Epps asked his graduate students to look at random dots, and then random numbers, on a projected computer screen. Most of the students saw patterns in both screens, even though the dots and numbers had been mathematically calculated to be random. We have all experienced the same thing when we have seen horses, faces, and castles in clouds. There are a number of cloud formation photographs on the Internet that people swear depict angels. Patients see figures and objects in psychologists' Rorschach inkblots. All this occurs because the human brain creates patterns where none exist.

Our own scientists have proven that physical matter is merely Energy vibrations that humans experience as solid matter. This is called "string theory" by physicists.[24]

During my afterlife experience, I was floored by the "knowings" that we Light Beings, together with Source, co-manifest what humans accept as reality. Human life feels so *real* while we are living it. Yet, while I was in the Light, I manifested physical realities for myself that felt as real as Earth life, except that I knew I was creating them with my thoughts. I knew then that I had been fooled into believing human life was real just by virtue of the fact that I did not know I was manifesting it.

You may wonder whether I am still fooled into accepting Earth life as real, now that I know the truth. Yes. It still feels absolutely real to me. Even though I know for certain that human life is purely manifested thought-forms, I get just as caught up in it now as I did before my beyond death experience. I am glad that I do, because that is what Source intended.

*　*　*

Question 2: What part of the brain do we use to manifest reality?

Discussion: No part of the brain can manifest. No part of the heart. No part of the human body at all is capable of manifesting reality. Manifesting is an innate spiritual ability we have as Beings of Light. It is not a human animal ability.

*　*　*

Question 3: How do we create physical reality?

Discussion: Manifesting requires two actions: "attention and intention." Focusing on something, giving it your attention, is the first part of the manifesting formula.

Attention can take a lot of different forms. It can involve thinking, visualizing, reading, or even talking about something. I have found the most powerful and effective form of attention is actually doing the legwork necessary to produce what I want. For example, if I wanted a new job, I would go out and look for one. I would get on the Internet and check out job search sites. I would talk to my friends who might have job openings. I would watch the news, talk to placement services, and maybe sign up for a while with a temp agency to get a feel for what kinds of jobs are out there. I could also take placement exams to identify my job skills and interests. All this legwork focuses powerful and consistent attention on securing a job. It also positions me to find one.

The second half of the manifesting formula is "intention." We must intend to experience as physical reality the thoughts we are projecting. We must have Light Being "creative" intent. While I was in the afterlife, I manifested various physical scenes that I had expected to see there. Expectation is a powerful form of intention.

During my life review, I remembered every single second of my life as Nanci, and all the sensory data my body had absorbed. I intended to share all that with my Light Being friends. So I did. All my experiences appeared as a unified whole visual memory all around me. Memories manifested into physical reality so that my friends could live them too.

We manifest instantly when we are out-of-body or in the afterlife. Attention and intention converge so quickly there appears to be no time lag at all between our thought and experiencing it as physical reality.

Manifesting is not instant when we inhabit human bodies. Every once in a while our manifesting efforts do produce results very quickly. You may say, "I'd really like to talk to Judy," and she calls within minutes. Or you might think, "I need a parking space right by the grocery store's front door that's not a handicap spot." Then, when you pull into the parking lot, you discover a perfect parking space right where you want it to be.

Generally, we cannot tell whether we have, in fact, manifested reality unless and until we see in hindsight that something we wanted to happen did happen.

✳   ✳   ✳

Question 4: How do we keep from manifesting random thoughts?

Discussion: Some writers on the topic of the law of attraction seem to fear random thoughts. They warn us to monitor our thinking at all times to avoid untoward manifestations. That concern is unfounded, based upon the "knowings" about manifesting I received during my beyond death experience.

Even while I was in the Light, if I had a random thought, it did not manifest into physical reality. I spent several seconds missing chocolate. No chocolate appeared. I remembered warm breezes on my face. No breezes manifested. I thought about rain falling on my head. No rain fell in the Light.

We do not have to be careful what we think every second for fear that we might manifest all kinds of random events. We only manifest what we intend to experience. Manifesting requires focused *spiritual* attention and intention. Random human thoughts do not satisfy these prerequisites.

✳   ✳   ✳

Question 5: How do we keep from manifesting negative thoughts into physical reality?

Discussion: I have read books, and heard speakers, who say the universe does not know the difference between "I want" and "I don't want." They claim we must be careful what we think because once a thought forms in our mind it will manifest, regardless of whether we do or do *not* want it. For example, one famous researcher cautions us not to have thoughts such as, "I don't want it to rain," because we will manifest rain. The "don't" part of the thought, to her, is irrelevant.

This view of manifesting ignores the "intention" part of the equation. It also assumes the manifesting power to be out there in the universe somewhere. *We* are the power behind manifesting. And *we* know the difference between what we want and what we do not want. There is no magic manifesting genie floating in space who does not understand the meaning of the word "not." Nor does Source fail to understand English. Once again, manifesting requires focused attention and intention. Random negative thoughts are not a concern.

Thinking negative thoughts does not attract negativity. We do not attract anything from the universe to ourselves, despite the literature on the so-called law of attraction. We manifest into reality, from our innate power as a Being of Light, the experiences on which we focus our attention and intention. We are co-creators with Source of our reality—not passive magnets of universal debris.

That is not to say that negative thoughts do not manifest. They do—if we have focused our attention on them with the intention that they manifest.

How many times have you said to yourself, "I was afraid this would happen?" If we truly are afraid, and focus our attention on that one fearful thought over a sustained period of time, we can manifest what we fear into reality.

For example, our body might be preoccupied with a fear—say, of a heart attack—and that fear will force our attention to the concern. We start looking for data to confirm or disprove the possibility that the feared event may materialize. The more medical tests we have run on the heart that show any small abnormality, the more convinced we become that the heart attack fear may be justified. The more facts seem to confirm the fear, the more we believe it will happen.

Although we do not specifically intend to have a heart attack, the second part of the manifesting formula is satisfied by our intention to focus Energy on that problem. Focusing a significant amount of attention and intention on a fear can manifest it into reality. *But only if we truly believe it can happen!* We have to believe we will have a heart attack for it to manifest. Fear alone will not do it.

Manifesting follows beliefs. We manifest what we truly and deeply believe about our world and ourselves, including our unknown beliefs. That is the catch! Most people think they know themselves. But few have enough introspection to even suspect their unconscious beliefs. In the above example, we could manifest the heart attack because we have an unconscious belief that heart trouble is in our genes. That is why it is so terribly important to become enlightened about our own beliefs. We cannot hope to manifest happier lives if we have no idea that we harbor beliefs that contradict our desire to be happy.

*   *   *

Question 6: Can we manifest bad things to happen to someone else?

Discussion: People have asked me whether damning someone to hell will actually cause them to go to hell. No. First, there is no hell. Second, mean thoughts about others do not change their lives (unless, of course, we act on those thoughts).

We cannot create someone else's reality, only our own. We manifest only for ourselves. We do, however, co-create reality with other Light Beings, with their permission. But we cannot do it without their permission and cooperation.

Example: Suppose a young man, Joe, thinks he wants to go to college, but he is uncertain. His father had told Joe all his life that his own dream was for his son to come into the family car repair business after finishing high school. All his teachers had always told Joe that he was not college material. When Joe started his senior year in high school, he was still conflicted about college. He thought he really wanted to go, despite others' opinions. Joe confided in his best friend, Dean, who mounted a campaign of making fun of Joe's college dream. Joe ended up going into the auto repair business with his father.

Did Dean prevent Joe from going to college by constantly expressing negative thoughts about it? Did Joe fail to effectively manifest his college desire by not giving it enough "attention and intention?"

Joe did not miss out on college because of Dean's negative thoughts or words because they were not creative in nature. Not all thoughts have creative power. Random thoughts, even negative ones, do not manifest either for us or in concert with others. We have to give creative power to our thoughts through focused spiritual attention and intention to manifest reality. Joe's friend did not manifest Joe's future. No one can manifest Joe's life but him and Source. Anyone involved in co-creating with Joe must agree at the Light Being level of awareness to do so.

Joe did not incompletely manifest his college dream, causing his efforts to fail. Joe did, in fact, manifest as he intended. He manifested what he truly believed: that he was not going to go to college. That is the thought to which Joe gave his undivided attention. And the result followed his subconscious intention to prove his teachers were right about him. This is another example of why it is so important for us to become aware of our own emotional issues and self-destructive beliefs and resolve them. Joe might have changed the direction of his life had he faced his poor self-image and changed his beliefs about his abilities before senior year in high school.

Alternatively, perhaps Joe chose this particular human life to test how he would respond to his father, teachers, and friends disparaging his dreams. He may have wanted to see whether he could successfully stay on his soul's chosen mission despite self-doubt, lack of support, and lack of advantages others sometimes get in human life, such as a college education.

Question 7: Why can't we manifest the material things we want?

Discussion: Manifesting reality is a spiritual ability. It is something we do as Light Beings invested into human bodies. Manifesting does not follow human desire. It follows what we souls believe is appropriate for our chosen hosts and the experiences we seek through them. We use manifesting in furtherance of our goals as spiritual beings, not human greed. Not a single soul on Earth really needs or wants a car, a house, a bracelet, or a pile of money. Material goods are irrelevant to a spiritual life. So we do not manifest them at the will of our hosts.

If we have manifested material goods into our life, it is because they are part of the lifestyle we have chosen this time. If we chose life in a monastery, we could contemplate the law of attraction until the cows come home and still not manifest a jet, a 125-foot yacht, or winning the lottery, because that would be inconsistent with our lifestyle. The life plan is chosen by the soul, not the body. We can consciously manifest those things and events that further our evolutionary goals, fit with the lifestyle we have chosen, and are consistent with the human being whose life we have decided to share.

✳ ✳ ✳

Question 8: When people say they have tried manifesting and it didn't work, why didn't it?

Discussion: Manifesting always works—every single second of our lives. We are constantly co-manifesting everything around us. Everything we see, hear, smell, and perceive is manifested by us, those co-creating with us, and Source. Manifesting always works.

When people say they tried to manifest a new car, boat, home, job, etc. and it did not work, what they mean is that their conscious efforts to manifest did not produce the immediate results they desired. How does that happen when manifesting always works?

There can be many reasons. Manifesting follows beliefs and unknown beliefs may have controlled the outcome. There can be a significant time lag between intention to manifest and seeing the results in the physical world. Maybe their attention was not focused, or they had not formed the creative intention. What they wanted to produce may not have fit with their life plan. They may not be able to recognize what they manifested. They may not realize that they were the ones responsible for a certain event.

Keep trying. The more we consciously harness our creative power, the more likely we are to manifest from our Light Being level of awareness, rather than unconscious beliefs.

Part III −What Happens When We Die?

Part III of *BACKWARDS: Returning to Our Source for Answers* starts with a chapter summarizing the various stages we pass through in the afterlife as we make our transition from sharing a human being's life to resuming our Light Being splendor. Subsequent chapters detail the chronological events of my beyond death experience in 1994, where I obtained the information contained in this two-volume set.

Part III of this *Guidebook* adds more detail to the description of what happens in the afterlife. And it adds new details to my beyond death experience chronology, as well as a description of how my life changed after returning to this world. Part III of this volume should be read in conjunction with Part III of *BACKWARDS*.

13

✳ Death as a Process

WHAT HAPPENS WHEN WE die? We already know but have forgotten. We are intimately familiar with the early stages of death because they replay in physical life morning after morning as a gentle reminder. We call the process "waking up." Death is but an awakening from a lower level of consciousness to a far grander one. A side-by-side comparison of the features of waking from sleep with awakening at death more clearly shows this correlation.

Abandoning the body is similar to the first moments of leaving the sleep state.

Sleep	Death
Upon departing dreamland, we experience a sudden jump in consciousness. One moment we are sound asleep, unconscious to our surroundings,	Upon death of the body, we experience a sudden jump in consciousness. One moment we are deeply ensconced in flesh, and the next we are

and the next we find ourselves in the physical world. We become aware that we are in a human body that has awakened from sleep.	floating freely with no physical form. We become aware that we have left the body but are still alive.

Just as we sometimes fight waking up, because it is too early or we are still tired, some souls resist the awakening process begun at death.

Sleep	Death
No matter how long we play possum, pretending to be asleep or trying vainly to get back to sleep, once we awaken we cannot soon return to dreams. So, instead of snuggling backwards into the cocoon of delta waves, we open our eyes to the light of day while still blanketed in the safety and warmth of bed. If someone tried to communicate with us at this stage we would sound groggy and incoherent,	No matter how long we play possum, and some souls do pretend they are still in the body and vainly try to continue physical life, once our host has died, and our connection to it is permanently broken, we cannot return to human life. So instead of hovering around our former body, we face forward into the safety and all-embracing love of the Light. If someone could communicate

saying things that make no sense.	with us at this stage, we would likely relate our out-of-body sensation in purely human terms because that is the only context we have within which to make sense of what happened.

Going into the Light is like a full body version of opening our eyes to daylight or the artificial light of a lamp. Reality begins to creep in as we exercise our mental faculties.

Sleep	**Death**
Soon after opening our eyes, we begin to orient to our surroundings and reclaim a physical identity. Our thoughts may lazily turn to, "It's Wednesday. I have to get up." Someone talking to us at this stage would most likely get an oriented response. "I'm awake. I'm getting up."	Soon after entering the Light, we begin to orient to our surroundings while interacting from habit as though still in a human body. We would most likely observe Earth-like surroundings that have been manifested to ease the transition. If someone could communicate with us at this stage, he/she would most likely get an Earth-oriented response. "I

	see trees and flowers and hear babbling brooks. It is so beautiful."

Eventually, we must all come to the realization that the event we call death has occurred, and accept that we are still alive and conscious, just as we must realize that a new day of human life has begun when the alarm clock calls us to the waking world.

Sleep	**Death**
Once the fog of sleep lifts completely, our thoughts may turn to the previous day's events or to tasks of the day ahead. "Ugh, I wish I hadn't eaten that pizza for dinner. I have to remind [spouse] to stop at the dry cleaners on the way to work. The kids need lunch money." Perhaps a child's voice or screech from the alarm clock pulls us farther into the day ahead. Our verbal responses at this stage would probably reflect our "to do"	Some souls do not realize they are dead until they see others who have passed on before them. So Light Beings take on the physical appearances of our deceased loved ones to welcome us and cue us to the fact that we have died. As we realize that we have left human life behind, our thoughts might turn to all we have lost. This could trigger a life review. If humans were able to communicate with us at this stage, our responses would be

list.	couched in terms of remembered past Earthly events.

Once fully awakened, we climb out of bed and begin the business of living life another day. Similarly, once we acknowledge that human life has passed, and we are in the "afterlife," we begin the business of resuming spiritual life as a Being of Light. This is the point where the waking process so familiar in human life departs radically from spiritual awakening.

In the Light, we remember not only our just passed human life but also all of our "past lives" in various physical and nonphysical forms. We recall that the answers to all of our questions about life and death are common knowledge. We know that all we need to do is focus our "attention and intention" on a particular subject to access Universal Knowledge of it. In short, we remember who and what we really are—spectacular living extensions of Source's own self-awareness.

Whether we believe in an afterlife, and how that existence might appear to us, may depend upon our religious and culturally ingrained opinions. These beliefs will most likely be flavored by the emotional stew that has become our way of responding to the world. For example, our childhood church may have taught that heaven exists. But if our parents forced religion on us as a form of control, we may have rebelled against religious teachings in protest over our parents' behavior. Adult experiences likewise temper our spiritual beliefs, perhaps changing them dramatically from childhood views.

The following questions are designed to elicit your firmly held beliefs about what happens after death and to give you a broader perspective on the afterlife.

*   *   *

Question 1: Which of the following do you believe survives death of the human body?

a. physical appearance

b. personality

c. memories

d. grief and a sense of loss

e. fear and anger

f. concern for the future

g. religious beliefs

h. bonding with family

i. worry about the past

j. concern for the living

Discussion: *Physical appearance.* Little has been written about the type of appearance we might have in the afterlife. A few texts speak of a spiritual "body" of varying densities of light glowing in hues from white to royal purple.[25] Some people believe the human body reconstitutes from decay to join the soul in heaven after the end of the world.

My personal experience was that *for a while* my five spiritual soul mates and I did appear to have a type of luminescent humanoid shaped "body." But that perception disappeared after I completed the transition into Light Being state. Thereafter, all six of us existed in a purely conscious but bodiless state.

Personality. Near-death experiencer reports, including my own, confirm that nearly all of our familiar personality traits survive death. My memories and thought processes were all still with me. My consciousness remained completely intact in the Light. I *recognized* myself in spiritual form as the same person I had been in the body.

Everything we hold dear as constituting our "self"—our likes, dislikes, sense of humor, and behavior quirks—everything that allows our loved ones to recognize us, continues on after death of the human host. Some aspects of human life, such as physical appearance and human family relationships, last only for so long as we need them in order to feel comfortable with the transition. Just as medical professionals would not tell a coma patient the instant he comes out of the coma that he has lost his entire family in an auto accident, our lovingly designed awakening process does not deprive us of all we once held dear until we are ready to relinquish it.

After we enter the Light, our essence is greatly enriched through infusions of unconditional love and acceptance. Moreover, the "knowings" we gain through contact with Universal

Knowledge, and as a result of reviewing our just passed human life, heal many of the defense mechanisms we generated in response to the pain and trauma of physical life. The end result is that we will still be ourselves, but healed and magnificent beyond our wildest dreams.

Our former human host's personality, however, does cease to exist. We may notice its loss. I did. Human character traits and beliefs based on fear will disappear because there is no fear in our spiritual home. All survival and mortality concerns evaporate. And human self-centeredness is replaced with a universality orientation once we realize we are all one in Source.

Memories. Our memories are eternal. In later stages of the transition from human life, the Energy we call "soul" rejoins the rest of our Light Being Energy, allowing us to remember our eons of living. Not only will we be able to recall every single second of the just concluded human life, along with every sensory input the body experienced, but we will remember that we have lived many other physical lives. We have also lived in nonphysical form as a Light Being between physical lives. We will remember who we really are–immortal beings composed of Source's own Energy and self-awareness. These memories will fulfill us and complete us in ways we may have sought our entire human lives.

Grief and loss. Feelings of grief and loss are not confined to human existence, though we experience far too much of them while in the body. We continue to be emotional beings after death.

But the emotions that predominate will shift from sorrow to love, peace, and joy.

Yet, human-like emotions may persist for a short while after death, depending upon how quickly we adjust to life in spirit form. The early stages of the transformation require us to realize that we have left human life behind, to acknowledge that we have experienced what humans call "death" and all that word implies. Coming to grips with this truth may generate a sense of grief and loss. And, from personal experience, I can say that some of us resist believing we have passed on.[26] This is particularly true when death came unexpectedly. Resisting the transition may prolong the sense of loss.

Grief and loss may also overtake those souls who fear judgment, or who were locked in the throes of violence or intense pain at the time their human host died. The emotional pain resulting from traumatic death, and the experiences the soul manifests because of that pain, have been alluded to in our religious myths as purgatory or hell.

Fear and anger. Our new emotional makeup in the Light exudes joy and bliss, replacing our former underlying current of fear. Fear is purely animal in origin. Perhaps fear had been so pervasive in human life that we became immune to feeling it. After death, all fear is gone. We will relish its absence, and feel the relief. Gone too will be all the mechanisms of bodily survival: breathing, heart beating, hunger, and the need for sleep. Gone is the fear that any day these constant reminders that we are alive might cease.

Once fear, physical pain, and illness evaporate, a good deal of anger dissipates with them. Often our anger has been a response to these primary stimuli. Anger directed toward other people will be resolved as part of the life review process, as will self-directed anger. But, speaking from my own experience, we still appear to be capable of a type of anger as Light Beings. I recall the serenity with which I accepted the answers to all my questions about life and death as they flowed to me from Universal Knowledge, only to be followed immediately by anger that the truth had been withheld from me during human life. My anger was not, of course, directed toward another being. Rather, it was more of a righteous indignation over the suffering we endure in human form at our own hands because we cannot remember who we really are. And *no one tells us.*

Future. A sense of linear time, including past and future, disappears once we leave physical matter. Shortly after I entered the Light, I discovered that many familiar human-life barriers had been removed—scientific laws, intellectual limitations, time, and space parameters. Time no longer existed for me, similar to how an artist loses awareness of the passage of time while painting, or a runner does in "runner's high." I saw time as irrelevant outside the body. It is merely an artificial system of measurement devised for man's convenience, like inches and pounds, which attempts to quantify units of experience into linear progression. There is no linear progression in the Light and no need to mark time. It is not that time stands still as humans understand that term; it simply does not exist as a barrier to accessing events or information.

Also, in the Light there are no external cues to give the illusion of time passing. All I saw was unbroken, unending illumination. What makes it seem time is passing on Earth is our observation of many life cycle processes, like plants sprouting and dying, the changing seasons, and our bodies' aging. Similarly, we watch the sun rising, setting, and traversing the sky, and adopt that rhythmic march to mark the progression of what we call time. Time, or marking time, or the orderly progression of events over time, is something unique to beings of matter. We no longer need it in spiritual form.

I have read much in scientific literature, not to mention fiction, about time and whether it can be abridged, slowed down, or revisited from the past or future. Now I see those experiments and theories as interesting, yet doomed to failure by the nature of the human being. Human bodies cannot get outside of time to accurately examine it. If they could, they would unmask time as the fiction it is. It is not a universal constant.

We will no longer care about the future after we die, for we will live ever after in the glory of the continuous now. All of eternity is ours to claim in the present moment. All can be experienced and known through attention and intention. There can be no anxiety about the future because no time period exists that we cannot know intimately now.

Religious beliefs. Religion is manmade. It does not survive death because actual knowledge replaces beliefs.

Family ties. Our concept of human animal family ties loses its importance to us in the afterlife. We realize that family bloodline is an animal concept and that spiritually we are all equally intimately related as part of Source. Our love for those Light Beings who have played the roles of our human family members does not decrease. Nor does their importance to us. But we no longer regard them as important to us *just because* they are family. Their stature in our eyes is elevated to one of pure love unrelated to their human roles. We are grateful they agreed to share the physical phase of their evolution with us. We may even discover one or more of them to be an eternal soul mate—someone whose very existence has been tied to ours forever. But, in the afterlife, we do not favor our former family members over the rest of creation, as we once did when we believed we were human.

I personally experienced something like family or kinship with my five Light Being friends, none of whom had been related to my human host. This connection was a sensation beyond family ties on Earth–deeper, more intimate, more acutely like I was a part of my friends in a literal sense. Some might call my Light Being friends "soul mates." That term fits pretty well.

Worry over the past. Religious dogma may cause us to worry about how we will be judged at death. That worry is unnecessary.

There is no judgment. No punishment. We will, however, have the opportunity to review every moment of our human life objectively with spiritual eyes full of unconditional love. The life review may be uncomfortable if we do not like how we behaved in human life. But the understanding and appreciation for others will completely overshadow the emotional pain. We will see that each second of time on Earth was precious and contributed so much to our evolution and awareness. We will learn how our behavior and words affected others, what could have happened had we made other choices, and what we should do next time to show unconditional love. We will forgive ourselves. Guilt will disappear as acceptance and loving understanding flood our hearts.

Concern for those left behind. It is the self-centeredness of the human condition that allows us to believe we will still be concerned with Earth life after we have left it. Once exposed to the tremendous love and knowledge of our spiritual state, concern for those on Earth will disappear. Worry is replaced by "knowings." We will know that while the soul part of our loved ones' Energy may still be in human bodies, the rest of their Energy is with us in the afterlife. In other words, we do not leave anyone behind. This concept is discussed in more detail in response to the next Question.

Human Perspective	Light Being Perspective	Source's Perspective
I assume I will still be very human-like, with human concerns, in the afterlife.	I am not human and will not have human concerns in the afterlife. I will resume my eternal Light Being identity and powers.	The afterlife is merely one state of a-wareness that my facets or extensions (i.e., Light Beings) experience. As they transition to greater awareness, they will understand human life to be a mani-festation or illusion.

✳   ✳   ✳

Question 2: Do you believe you will see your human loved ones "on the other side?"

Discussion: One of the most cherished memories a near-death experiencer relates upon returning from the Light is that of having been reunited with deceased loved ones. I did not see any of my human life loved ones who had passed.[27] But, I did learn about this phenomenon during my beyond death experience by focusing upon it while I had full access to Universal Knowledge. The truth revealed to me is startling, yet oddly reassuring.

The "knowings" I received can be divided into the different levels of understanding represented by human perspective, Light Being perspective, and Source's ultimate perspective.

Human Perspective	Light Being Perspective	Source's Perspective
I assume the afterlife is a place and that my loved ones will appear to be human there.	We invest only part of our total Energy into a human animal as its "soul." The remainder of our Energy stays in the Light. I am always in the company of my loved ones because they are still in the Light with me while some of their Energy has taken soul form.	I am the only Being in this universe. All other "beings" are my manifestations. I am omnipresent. So, to the extent that other beings seem to exist, they exist everywhere all the time, the same as I do.

Human perspective. While we occupy human bodies we have only their frame of reference—unless we make the effort to become enlightened. We souls typically think like humans rather than Light Beings. We consent to be limited to the human perspective as part of the adventure.

Humans perceive a physical world with biological senses and assume that limited type of experience extends into the afterlife as well. It does not. The common belief that we continue to appear as human beings in the afterlife is understandable, but erroneous. Although Light Beings do have the capability of donning any look we wish, we do not routinely project a human appearance. Not routinely. Some Light Beings do assume the form of our Earthly loved ones to help us through the transition process. They are not trying to deceive us, but rather to convey love and guidance in a form we recognize. When near-death experiencers see their deceased loved ones in the Light, they may have been reunited with Light Beings who used to be their Earthly loved ones. Or, unknown Light Beings whose job it is to assist with the transition process might have welcomed the NDEr with a comforting appearance.

Light Being perspective. When we die, we do not literally "go" anywhere. We simply expand our consciousness and resume enjoying life at multiple simultaneous levels of awareness. Consequently, we never actually leave the physical world, any more than we were ever truly in it. The physical universe is another vibration within Source's thoughts, not something separate from it or us. All that is required to bridge the gap from physical to spiritual level, then, is a change in focus, an alteration in our "attention and intention."

In our natural spiritual state we are capable of living on multiple levels of consciousness at the same time. Even though we may have invested one level of our self-awareness into a human body, our other levels of perception remain in the Light and continue to evolve there. All of us who are experiencing the human adventure are still in the Light—with each other. In truth, our departed loved ones are always right there beside us—a mere level of awareness away.

It is Source's gift to us, and itself, that we enjoy the illusion of separation from Source and each other. But it is just an illusion. It seems very real to us while in human bodies because of the limitations and restrictions imposed by physical matter. Physical bodies "dumb us down" to the point that we forget entirely who we are and the powers we hold. But we can break the illusion of separateness and connect with each other across awareness levels. We can communicate with our loved ones at any level of awareness—human or divine—by focusing our "attention and intention" on making contact. It takes considerable effort for most of us while in a human body, but the ability comes more easily once we resume spiritual form.

We are capable of this shift from one level of awareness to another whether in physical or spiritual form. You may have sensed the presence of a deceased loved one. Or you heard a sound, smelled a fragrance, or saw something that reminded you of someone and gave you the "knowing" that they were close.

Our deceased loved ones may also sense our closeness and wish to initiate communication but cannot. The transition from human existence to divine takes what we would perceive to be time, and which souls perceive to be developmental stages. Souls undergoing this transfiguration are fully engaged in it and are generally unaware of anything else. That does not mean they have forgotten their loved ones. They are busy within a spiritual process that must be completed as surely as our bodies' survival tasks must be performed. When they reach a level where they are able to, and interested in, communicating with loved ones still in the body, they will do so in various ways. *Hello From Heaven!* by Bill and Judy Guggenheim[28] recounts hundreds of true stories of after-death communications between Light Beings and humans.

Source's perspective. Source is the only Being in this universe. All so-called "beings" constitute only one collective entity, Source. All creatures ultimately exist solely within Source's imagination. What seems to separate us from Source and each other is simply lack of awareness of our origin as Source's thoughts. We cannot perceive each other's presence within Source's mind, similar to how a patient under anesthesia during surgery is unaware that the surgeon and nurses surround him.

Source exists everywhere at all times. To the extent that we seem to individually exist within Source's mind, then, each and every one of us is everywhere all the time, just as Source is.

Therefore: everyone is everywhere all the time.

* * *

Everyone is everywhere all the time.

The importance of this startling statement is that it means we do not have to wait until our human hosts die before we can communicate with loved ones who have left this plain of awareness. We can sense them, feel their presence, bathe in their love, and receive messages via mental telepathy while still in the body. We are not alone.

The bond of love that connects us is strong enough to bridge the communication gap if we open enough to allow it. Sometimes all that is required is that we relax our grip on grieving. We cannot feel others' emotions, even love, while we are drowning in our own. Sometimes we must be still. We cannot hear others' words when our minds are full of thoughts. And, we need to be able to feel. We cannot feel another's presence if we have numbed ourselves to all but a chosen few sensations.

Death is a frightening prospect for humans. But we are not humans. We are spiritual beings able to navigate the currents and eddies of a multitude of awareness states. All we have to do is awaken to the knowledge of who we really are. Begin your journey of awakening now.

14

Nanci's Death

I died March 14, 1994.

Alone, and waiting to be taken over to the cancer hospital for surgery, I slipped out of my body while no one was looking. The radiologist, who had performed a pre-surgery invasive procedure on my right breast, left a few minutes before I did. She went only so far as down the hall. I, on the other hand, catapulted into the most glorious adventure ever—the afterlife.

Leaving the Body. Some internal alarm alerted me that my body was failing. My eyesight was the first deserter. My vision sputtered and ultimately blinked out like a fluorescent lamp. I experienced tunnel vision before complete darkness, but did not behold any tunnel leading to the Light. Hearing abandoned me next. Soon, "I" was sinking within my own body. I literally took off my body as though it were clothes. The sensation approximated taking off a thick, heavy, tight wetsuit, but without the work of manipulating limbs around. Of course, at first, I did not believe I was *leaving* my body—only that I was blacking out. Yet, I never lost consciousness. I felt totally wide-awake and aware. Clearly something other than fainting had me in its grips.

After standing literally in front of my own sitting body, I slid into darkness. This blackness was more tactile than visual. I could sense unseen others. There were no sounds. No pounding heartbeat to pierce the silence. No physical mass to support me.

The black void occupied space or a dimension similar to it. It lasted only a moment though it seemed infinite by nature. Blazing into the void was a pinprick of Light in the distance. I recognized the phenomenon as normal, and thought to myself: "Oh, yeah, I know what this is. I'm supposed to go into the Light." Going into the Light seemed the natural direction to head, like turning into my driveway from the street fronting my house. And while it occurred to me that I had gone through this process many times before, I did not mentally connect it to death. I was not the least bit concerned about life or death because it was clear I was *not dead!*

My passage from darkness to Light was quick, accomplished via an entirely mental sense of motion quite unlike walking or floating. Forward projection resulted from merely shifting my focus to the Light.

In the Light. Upon first glimpse, the lighted area seemed to have dimensions in space. Once inside it, though, I realized it had no physical properties. "Light" is simply how humans perceive this higher level of Energy. A glorious, warm, embracing, and loving sensation full of acceptance and welcome enveloped me in the Light. Then, I literally *became* the Light.

I was alone in the Light. There were no sounds and nothing to see. I felt nothing resembling physical matter. There was nothing to do. But I was totally entertained by the explosion of thoughts and emotions.

I was relieved to discover I had survived the passage from human life to heaven completely intact. This surprised me. Though I had been indoctrinated by religion, and believed, that I have a soul, it had never occurred to me before that moment that what I called "soul" was an entire being—ME. I had always thought my soul was part of my human self; I thought I was a human being with an immortal soul. But I discovered in the Light that I am not human at all. I merely share a human's body and life with her. And each of us is a separate consciousness, though we coexist within one body.

A full understanding of humans and our relationship to them suddenly appeared in my mind from out of nowhere.[29] I learned humans are wonderful, sophisticated Earth animals we silently inhabit. We are so intimately enmeshed with our hosts since before their births that humans are not even aware they are inhabited by spiritual beings. At most, humans perceive us as simply part of them—as their consciences or souls.

Many, many other insights bombarded me while I basked in the

Light. Thoughts seemed to have a life of their own. "Knowings" flooded my mind on the subjects of psychology, physics, the difference between human animals and who we really are as spiritual beings,[30] and how foolishly I had lived my life and how to correct that. [31]

A series of "knowings" on how humans treat mental illness saddened me. I understood that animals cull from the herd those members whose weaknesses threaten group safety. That is how humans perceive mental illness—as a threat to the herd. Mentally ill persons are culled from society either physically through institutionalization or emotionally through social stigma. I regarded such attitudes as not only ignorant but also primitive. Many conditions classified as abnormal are actually the result of a soul being able to exhibit some of its spiritual abilities through the body.

For example, people called savants are simply displaying more of their innate spiritual nature than others typically do. Persons with uncanny factual memories or mathematical skills (like the character in the movie *Rainman*) are exhibiting the total recall common to us all in our Light Being state. Uncommon musical ability likewise is a display of innate creativity we share with Source.

Humans label multiple personalities as a mental disorder, instead of recognizing the phenomenon as an expression of a higher state of being. Having multiple personas is normal for Light Beings. We have all lived many, many physical lifetimes as different people, each of whom exhibited a unique personality. Those personalities integrate into our one true identity as an eternal being.

A deeper understanding of sexuality shockingly entered my mind unbidden, while I was living in the Light. Suddenly, I knew for certain that sex is not a bad or evil sensation to be avoided or tamed, as sixteen years of religious education had implied. It is simply one of the many delights of being in a body and should be explored and enjoyed for what it is. Sex has no more significance than that. Human beings are prized as hosts partly because of the thrill of sexual expression and physical loving they offer. Sexuality affords a unique opportunity to relate to one another in a primal, yet oddly spiritual, way. The spiritually of sex emerges when partners share a moment of true love for each other in this most vulnerable of states.

Wonderful new mental abilities enthralled me in the Light. They included total recall, instant and complete understanding of any subject, the ability to hold multiple simultaneous levels of awareness, and the ability to instantly manifest what we call physical reality.

The closest analogy to multiple simultaneous levels of awareness in human life might be multi-tasking. For example, assume you are both reading the paper and watching a game on TV. Although you miss part of the game when you read, you are still able to capture its highlights, along with the gist of everything you read. You have split your attention between two activities. Now imagine that instead of being split, your attention has doubled. You can both read the paper and watch TV without losing a moment of either. Finally, rather than simply multi-tasking, imagine you are one mind spread across two clones, each of whom you observe as though looking at them from the outside. That is, you can see yourself watching TV, be aware that you are watching a football game, and know every detail of every play. Similarly, you witness yourself reading the paper, are aware that you are reading, and understand and recall every word. Moreover, you are doing all this at the same time. Such an experience would approach the sensation of multiple levels of awareness that I enjoyed in the Light, though I shifted among far more layers.

While experimenting with multiple simultaneous levels of awareness, something suddenly shifted my attention to my former body. I glimpsed it, down in the mammography room of the hospital, through the back of the head part of my new spiritual form. It was sitting just as I had left it—upright in the chair, arms resting on the chair arms, feet flat on the floor, breast wire sticking out of the hospital gown, and head straight and high. The body's blue-grey eyes were wide open and staring at the film view boxes at the back of the room.

I was surprised the body was not slumped over or limp from passing out. It looked alive to me. The strange thought crept into my mind that the body *was* still alive; it was possible for me to stay in the Light and for the body to recover and go on living without me. Unfortunately, I did not care enough about my former host to puzzle it further. I wish now that I had pursued the train of thought.

I was interested, however, in the fact that since I had left it, "my" body had become "the" body in my thinking. The body was no longer me. I had no more emotional attachment to it than to the chair holding it. Body. Chair. Floor. It all meant the same to me.

Observing my former body generated that sensation of multiple simultaneous levels of awareness. In one and the same instant, I was aware that: (a) I could see out of the back of what would be the head of a human body; (b) this vantage point would be perceived by a human as being at ceiling height; and (c) I was not really hovering at the ceiling and only had that perception because humans gauge distance visually. I was also simultaneously aware that: (d) I had no interest in the dearly departed human; (e) I was surprised by that lack of interest; and (e) I adjudged myself arrogant for lacking concern for a being that for forty-three years I had thought of as myself. These thoughts are all quite possible in the body, of course. But they would present in linear sequence rather than as a collective simultaneous whole understanding.

The visual observation that I had separated from the body still in the mammography suite was my first inkling that I might have died. "Nah, I can't be dead," I said to myself. I felt so incredibly alive! More alive than I had ever felt on Earth. "Besides," I reasoned, "I didn't go through a tunnel. I always heard you go through a tunnel into the Light when you die." Instantly I found myself in a tunnel. I knew the tunnel to heaven could not possibly be real because I had already been in the Light for a long time. "Knowings" came to me that I had manifested the tunnel by thinking of it in the belief that it was necessary to go through a tunnel in order to get to heaven. I tried manifesting other scenes to see if I could do it. I manifested a beautiful meadow as heaven and the corridor of the hospital where my surgery was being performed.

Seeing my body back on Earth forced an intellectual recognition that my body had died. Acknowledging that I had survived death seemed to be the key to moving beyond the empty illuminated area. I felt I had been alone in the Light long enough and was ready for something more.

Beings of Light. I became aware of five colored layers of light within the overall illumination. Their hues were exquisitely subtle in their differences—far too subtle for human eyes to distinguish. I knew they would translate into the color white if perceived through human vision. But to my spiritual vision, they were deliciously colorful, full of depth and meaning. I instinctively knew the colors' names in a language that sounded both ancient and foreign. I recognized the language as my native tongue.

The five layers of light within the Light receded enough for me to discern beings standing in front of them. The Beings had no bodies as such, but rather sketchy humanoid outlines. I could vaguely make out heads and shoulders, but no limbs. Their faces had no features. Their heads were bald. I sensed no age, race, sex, or other distinguishing characteristic. Not one of them was my long dead father or sister, nor my more recently deceased grandparents. Nor were these Beings extended family members, or anyone else I had ever known on Earth. My mind labeled them as "Energy Beings," for they seemed composed entirely of energy. I have since heard near-death experiencers call them Beings of Light and have adopted that term.

A sense of homecoming overpowered me as I beheld these Light Beings. I was finally HOME! An incredible wealth of "knowings" about my true Light Being nature inundated my mind. I understood more fully that I had inhabited a human body as a mode of experience and expression. It became clear to me that I had always been a Being of Light and Energy. All I knew to be true about ME continued to exist in my Light Being self, not in the body left back in the mammography room. All my thoughts, feelings, memories, understanding, knowledge, learning, and emotions—everything was still with me. I realized that what humans call a soul is in fact a Being of Light like those around me.

Armed with this new understanding, I found it incredible that I could ever have believed myself to be human. I felt like an ex-cult member who had been brainwashed and seduced by the human cult, only to learn once I was deprogrammed that it was all a lie. While living in Nanci, I believed whole-heartedly in everything I saw and heard. Human life was my reality—the only one I thought I would ever know. Once I knew the truth about eternal reality, however, I could not imagine ever again being fooled into believing I am human.

I instinctively communicated telepathically with the Beings. I recognized them and knew their names in the same foreign sounding language as the names of the colors. These Beings are my dearest, closest, most beloved eternal friends and companions.

The Life Review. Accompanied by my dear friends, I processed through a transformative experience that included replaying my entire human life for my friends' benefit. This life review is described in detail in *BACKWARDS: Returning to Our Source for Answers.* Sometime later, I realized that my life review included only the timeline I remembered as Nanci's life. Before this afterlife experience, I had believed there were multiple parallel universes, and, that I existed in more than one of them. I comforted myself with the belief that whatever life choices I failed to make in this universe would be chosen in my parallel lives. Sadly, I saw no parallel lives or universes during my life review. Nor did Universal Knowledge disclose to me any "knowings" about other universes.

The Memory Recapture. Superimposed over the life review was an event I call the "memory recapture." I can only describe it as reclaiming my full Energy Being memories and identity. I remembered possibly thousands of physical and non-physical lifetimes I had lived over eons of time. While recently reliving this portion of my after death transformation, I recalled living as a woman in Paris, France in the 1700s, and as a shuttle pilot on another planet where I transfer cargo from space dock into the holds of large space ships.

Access to Universal Knowledge. Upon becoming conscious that I had full access to the knowledge of the universe, I sought answers to all my existential questions. Those answers are detailed in Parts I of this book and the first *BACKWARDS* book.

One of the more surprising revelations from Universal Knowledge was that we Light Beings cannot invest all of our Energy into human beings as their souls. Human physical matter is too dense. Consequently, part of our Energy and identity remains in the Light while we pursue our human adventures. This connection creates a natural conduit for us to continue to access Universal Knowledge while in the body.

Nothing about the afterlife *I* lived fit the picture of heaven painted by my former religion. Intensely curious, I perused Universal Knowledge for an explanation for the lack of conformity to the religious model of the afterlife. In response, a documentary of the history of Earth, and the role religion has played in mankind's evolution, played out in my mind. That story forms the framework for the yet-to-be-published book entitled *BACKWARDS Beliefs*.

The Merger and Return. Once my Energy vibrated fast enough, my five Light Being friends and I merged together, then into Source. Joining Source allowed me to witness firsthand the creation of the universe and what it all meant. I intimately understood Source and my relationship to it. I was more sublimely happy than I had ever remembered being. Nevertheless, I was disquieted by the fact that I felt the simple truths of life and death had not been readily available to those of us suffering the amnesia of being in humans. So I decided to return to human life. I vowed to tell everyone who would listen that love is all that truly matters, love is our innate nature as part of Source, and the truths of life and death are crafted by Source in love, not fear.

I returned to the body waiting for me in the mammography room. I felt no respiration or heartbeat for several minutes—not until after the body's blood pressure began to rise. It was almost as though I could not fully integrate back into the flesh until blood sufficiently permeated all parts of it.

The surgery proceeded uneventfully thereafter. My host and I emerged from the cancer hospital with a clean bill of health.

More details of the chronology of my afterlife experience and return to the body appear in Chapters 20-22 of *BACKWARDS: Returning to Our Source for Answers.*

15

Aftermath

MY HOST BODY HAD no inkling that I had left her and entered the Light. The last thing she remembered was blacking out. The emotional reality that my body had actually *died* ripped through us both twenty months later while watching the TV movie *Saved by the Light*, the famous true story of near-death experiencer Dannion Brinkley. The depiction of Mr. Brinkley's return to heaven after his death from a lightning strike jolted me into exclaiming: "That's what happened to me! That's it! I knew I wasn't hallucinating." That is how my human host learned I had gone into the afterlife and returned.

Despite my seeming familiarity with dying while doing it, I had never heard of anyone dying and returning to life before I saw *Saved by The Light* in December 1995. I spent Christmas vacation that year reading books about near-death experiences, including several by Raymond Moody, M.D., and Melvin Morse, M.D. These books were extremely interesting, but none related a story as extensive or detailed as mine. However, validation that my experience was a known medical phenomenon encouraged me to accept it as real and act upon it.

The aftermath of my return to the body was apparently typical, judging from what I have read. Flitting back and forth between denying the experience and marveling at it, I consulted several physicians, each of whom assured me my "heaven" was just hallucinations from the blood pressure drop. Seeking understanding, I told my story to anyone who would listen. Most were polite enough not to roll their eyes until after I looked away. So, after a while, I stopped telling people.

I was initially high on the Universal Knowledge I had gained and the assurance that life did not end with human death. I was also depressed. More than anything I had ever wanted before in my whole life, I wanted to go back to the Light. I missed my beloved soul mates. I missed being loved unconditionally. I wanted to reunite with Source. For two full years, I grieved the loss of my spiritual Home, my Light Being friends, unconditional acceptance, Universal Knowledge, and supernatural powers.

Dying did, however, gave me the courage to do something I would never in a million years have considered otherwise. I left the security of my large prestigious law firm, and I hung out my shingle as a solo practitioner. The anxiety of wondering if I could make a living on my own was brutal. Yet I could not tolerate my old way of life. Knowing that the human measure of success gains you nothing in the afterlife made the silly little ego games I had played as a big firm lawyer unacceptable.

I started changing my life in other ways. I put more effort into overcoming the personality traits and faults that hurt other people. Now that I know I will have to relive every word and deed in my next life review, I work harder to be a more loving person. My family agrees I am warmer now. My former employees can attest to the difficulty, and varying degrees of success, of my efforts to break old habits and replace them with unconditional acceptance of others. Many times the task still defeats me.

A second, more memorable, life review gripped me a few years after I returned from death, as I sat meditating in a rocking chair in the sitting room adjoining my master bedroom. A semi-trance state crept over me slowly. Then, violently, I was flung full force into a review of this Earth life. I saw every single, teeny, tiny thing I had ever done. I listened to every word I had uttered or heard from birth to death. Each event played across my mind's movie screen with me cast not only as the main character, but also as every other person involved in the scene. I experienced life from each person's perspective and *felt* each one's emotions.

As one small example, I saw myself sitting at a conference table surrounded by other attorneys from my old law firm. The air was thick with tension among the associates (young attorneys who are employees before becoming partners) around me. I squirmed, restlessly crossing and re-crossing my legs out of boredom.

Unbeknownst to me, I accidentally kicked one of the associates across from me under the table. The young man was instantly flummoxed. He took my kick as a rebuke. He assumed I had caught him daydreaming and was privately reprimanding him for it under the table. He was humiliated—and I could *feel* it! Here I was just being careless with my feet, and a young lawyer was mortified that a partner had kicked him for losing interest in another partner's droning diatribe. My associate's humiliation stung me, for I had no idea that my mere inattention could hurt someone else.

I saw instances where I had uncharacteristically touched acquaintances on sunburned skin, causing them to believe I wanted to hurt them. Everyone knew I never touched other people in a business setting, except for handshakes. But, inexplicably, sunburn seemed to be a magnet for my hand. I could have smacked myself every time I saw an instance like this replayed because I had not intended harm. I sensed my victims could have smacked me too! I could feel their emotions, and hear their thoughts. It was not pretty.

This second life review featured so many mindless little flicks of my limbs that for a while afterwards I dreaded being around other people. I feared I would unintentionally harm someone else and have to experience that pain when I die again.

I was horrified that such small, unintended acts could be so prominent in my life review. My previous understanding had been backwards; I had believed only my intentional actions "counted."

223

This life review showcased the truth that every single moment of our lives has significance. All the unintended insults, all the unknowing slights, and all the absentminded words and deeds make us who we are, and help determine how we will experience the awakening we call the afterlife.

Another unique aspect of this life review was the fact that it included my future. Tremendous distress over future events caused me to do what I could to prevent their occurrence. So far, I have been successful in changing the course of my life as it was projected in 1997, which convinces me of our freedom of choice.

The most prophetic event I witnessed was near the end of my life, at age eighty-three. I vividly recall standing on a cliff overlooking the Pacific Ocean, looking southward along the mountainous shoreline. I knew the old coastline, and land between the mountains and the Pacific Ocean, had fallen into the sea. I shifted my gaze back to the Wellness Center where I was working. The Center was dedicated to healing, wellness, refuge, rejuvenation, spiritual guidance, and peace. It was one of many such centers all over the world, built after the catastrophes of 2013-2014. The Center had become a Mecca to people of all walks of life—a crossroads where life was explored more deeply and spirituality revered. The Centers, or at least recognition of their need, saved humankind from total destruction at the end of this, the Second Epoch.

I have recently learned that Dannion Brinkley, author of *Saved by the Light*,[32] had been led by his near-death experience visions to build a center like the one where I worked. Ned Dougherty, author of *Fast Lane to Heaven*,[33] was also instructed in his near-death experience to build a center like I saw in my future. I believe these Centers can literally change our lives if we are willing. They offer services that can put us in touch with who we really are. Center personnel can help lead us on a path of spiritual discovery.

After a few years, I was back in my old habits of working too long and hard and putting too much pressure on my employees and myself. Though my drive for recognition as a success had weakened, my taste for money had not. My goal was to retire at age fifty-two. So I worked, and worked, and worked myself almost into the grave again. In 2001, I became very ill with medical conditions that sent me to the Emergency Room three times. At one point, I developed very low blood sodium that necessitated a two-day hospital admission. My body nearly died twice. My planned retirement turned into a yearlong forced medical leave. The Light Being Council (see Chapter 10) had to intervene once again to remind me why I am really here.

For fourteen full years I have processed my beyond death experience, reading, writing, and going to support group meetings to be with others who have had similar experiences. Life after death from this world is never far from my mind.

16

Conclusion

NEAR-DEATH STUDIES RESEARCHERS would characterize my experience as transcendental, longer and more complicated than most, and centered on the human condition and solutions to life's problems, rather than anything strictly personal to my life. The personal aftereffect, however, was to emblazon upon my heart a guiding mission for the rest of this life. When I was ripped from merger with Source and propelled back into this body, I assigned myself the task of telling as many people as I can what I learned of our true nature and purposes on Earth.

One purpose is our collective duty to experience humanness on Source's behalf. We are extensions of Source's own self-awareness, its identity, and we co-create this Earth with our Source to order to feel the raw emotions and physicality of human animals.

Each of us has an individual mission to understand our true nature as a Light Being soul inhabiting a human being. We need to become aware of our intrinsic grandeur as part of Source. Despite the overwhelmingly constant emphasis in society on our hosts' importance, their lives are temporary manifestations. Despite a hundred religions' insistence that we are humans with souls, we are spiritual Beings who only inhabit humans. We share humans' lives, but not their fates. We live in this world, but are not of it. It is time we proudly acknowledge our place in creation.

We souls must awaken to our powers and use them to temper our hosts' destructive actions, so that the up-coming transition to the Third Epoch will not hinge again on global destruction of the human species. It was made clear to me, during my afterlife review of Earth's history, that the collective intentions of everyone on Earth would determine when and how the Second Epoch will end—like the first one did, with the planet's human population destroyed, or with a less intense and slower transition to an enlightened era of peace and harmony.

And, finally, we are here to improve the human condition while we tread these earthen paths. We do this by increasing unconditional love in our daily lives. This will help synchronize our bodies' vibrations with our own Energy signatures and reduce the conflict between the two personalities. Raising humans' vibration level would increase their happiness as matter-bound adventurers tenfold.

Ultimately, love is all that matters. Every near-death and afterlife experiencer returns with the same message—that love is the most important aspect of life. Dannion Brinkley's character, in the movie based on his book *Saved By The Light*, sums it up by saying: "We are all powerful spiritual beings, and love is the difference God makes." My own beyond death experience convinced me of the truth of Mr. Brinkley's statement. But applying that wisdom has never been as easy as repeating it. So here are a few simple guidelines that work for me: unconditional love means giving to others even when they do not know we have done so. Giving when it is impossible for others to appreciate it. Giving love unselfishly to all, at all times, for no reason at all.

NOTES

[1]   Deepak Chopra, MD and David Simon, MD, *Training the Mind; Healing the Body,* available on CD from Nightingale-Conant Corp.

[2]   Kurt Leland, *Otherwhere: A Field Guide to Nonphysical Reality for the Out-of-Body Traveler* (Charlottesville, VA: Hampton Roads Publishing Co. 2001), 31.

[3]   The June 24, 2008 Pew Forum on Religion and Public Life survey concluded that ninety-two percent of Americans believe in God or a universal spirit.

[4]   Neale Donald Walsch, *What God Wants: A Compelling Answer to Humanity's Biggest Question* (New York: Atria Books 2005), 83. Reprinted with the permission of ATRIA BOOKS, an imprint of Simon & Schuster Adult Publishing Group from WHAT GOD WANTS by Neale Donald Walsch. Copyright © 2005 by Neale Donald Walsch.

[5]   Walsch, *What God Wants,* 83, 87.

[6]   Nanci L. Danison, *BACKWARDS: Returning to Our Source for Answers* (Columbus, OH: A.P. Lee & Co., Ltd. 2007), 28.

[7]   Neale Donald Walsch, *Conversations with God: An Uncommon Dialogue,* Books 1 (New York: G.P. Putnam's Sons 1996), 170-171. From CONVERSATIONS WITH GOD: AN UNCOMMON DIALOGUE, BOOK 1 by Neale Donald Walsch, copyright © 1995 by Neale Donald Walsch. Use by permission of G.P. Putnam's Sons, a division of Penguin Group (USA) Inc.

[8]   Carlos H. Schenck, MD, *SLEEP: the Mysteries, the Problems, and the Solutions* (New York: Avery 2007), 1.

[9]   Kenneth Ring, PhD, *Lessons From the Light: What We Can Learn From the Near-Death Experience* (Needham, MA: Moment Point Press 2000), 158-159.

[10]   Kim Zapf, *Wake Up to Your Intuitive Path* (Lambertville, MI: self-published 2007), xix.

[11]   Eckhart Tolle, *The Power of Now: A Guide to Spiritual Enlightenment* (Novato, CA: New World Library/Namaste Publishing 1999).

[12]   Eckart Tolle, *A New Earth--Awakening to Your Life's Purpose* (New York: Dutton 2005), 55.

[13]   Schenck, 4, 197.

[14]   *See, generally,* Jacqueline Smith, *Animal Communication—Our Sacred Connection* (Lakeville, MN: Galde Press 2005).

[15]   Michael F. Roizen, MD and Mehmet C. Oz, MD, *YOU Staying Young: The Owner's Manual for Extending Your Warranty* (New York: Free Press), 73. Reprinted with the permission of The Free Press, a Division of Simon & Schuster, Inc. from *YOU: Staying Young: The Owner's Manual for Extending Your Warranty* Michael F. Roizen, MD and Mehmet C. Oz, MD. Copyright © 2007 by Michael F. Roizen, MD and Oz Works, LLC. All rights reserved.

[16]   Donald M. Epstein, DC, *Healing Myths, Healing Magic* (San Rafael, CA: Amber-Allen Publishing, Inc. 2000).

[17]   Danison, 115.

[18]   Eugene T. Gendlin, Ph.D., *Focusing* (New York: Bantam Books 1981), 32-33. From FOCUSING by Dr. Eugene T. Gendlin, copyright © 1978, 1981 by Eugene T. Gendlin, Ph.D. Used by permission of Bantam Books, a division of Random House, Inc.

[19]   Gendlin, 173-174.

[20]   Photo downloaded from Google, which lists the original source as www.mrhartanssciencclass.files.wordpress.com. Mr. Hartan's web page showing this photo could not be located.

[21]   Photo downloaded from Ted Bundy's MySpace web page.

[22]   Rhonda Byrne, *The Secret* (New York: Atria Books 2006).

23   Byrne, 49.

24   Don J. Feeney, Jr., *Motifs: The Transformative Creation of Self* (Westport, CT: Greenwood Publishing Group 2001), 26.

25   See, for example, Michael Newton, Ph.D.'s books *Journey of Souls: Case Studies of Life Between Lives* (St. Paul, MN: Llewellyn Publications 5th Revised Ed. 2001) and *Destiny of Souls: New Case Studies of Life Between Lives* (St. Paul, MN: Llewellyn Publications 5th Revised Ed. 2001).

26   Some colorful and very human-like perceptions of the early stages of transformation, including what he calls the "Immigration Zone", appear in Kurt Leland's books entitled *Otherwhere: A Field Guide to Nonphysical Reality for the Out-of-Body Traveler* (Charlottesville, VA: Hampton Roads 2001), 119-121; and *The Unanswered Question: Death, Near-death, and the Afterlife* (Charlottesville, VA: Hampton Roads 2002), 138 and elsewhere.

27   I did reunite with my soul mate "family." But none of them had been in a human body during my lifetime as Nanci, or for thousands of Earth years before that.

28   Bill Guggenheim and Judy Guggenheim, *Hello From Heaven!* (New York: Bantam Books 1995).

29   What I remember of these "knowings" appears primarily in Chapter 10 of *BACKWARDS: Returning to Our Source for Answers*.

30   Chapter 11 of *BACKWARDS: Returning to Our Source for Answers* describes most of what I learned during this phase of my beyond death adventure.

31   See Part II of *BACKWARDS: Returning to Our Source for Answers*.

32   Dannion Brinkley with Paul Perry, *Saved By The Light: The True Story of a Man Who Died Twice and the Profound Revelations He Received* (HarperCollins 1994).

33   Ned Dougherty, *Fast Lane to Heaven: A Life-After-Death Journey* (Charlottesville, VA: Hampton Roads 2001).

BIBLIOGRAPHY

Byrne, Rhonda, *The Secret.* New York: Atria Books, 2006.

Chopra, Deepak, MD, and David Simon, MD, *Training the Mind; Healing the Body.* Niles, IL: Nightingale-Conant, CD.

Danison, Nanci L., *Backwards: Returning to Our Source for Answers.* Columbus, OH: A.P. Lee & Co., Ltd., 2007.

Feeney, Jr., Don J., *Motifs: The Transformative Creation of Self.* Westport, CT: Greenwood Publishing Group, 2001.

Gendlin, Eugene T., PhD, *Focusing.* New York: Bantam Books, 1981.

Guggenheim, Bill and Judy Guggenheim, *Hello From Heaven!* New York: Bantam Books, 1995.

Leland, Kurt, *Otherwhere: A Field Guide to Nonphysical Reality for the Out-of-Body Traveler.* Charlottesville, VA: Hampton Roads Publishing Co., 2001.

Ring, Kenneth, PhD, *Lessons From the Light: What We Can Learn From the Near-death Experience.* Needham, MA: Moment Point Press, 2000.

Roizen, Michael F., MD and Mehmet C. Oz, MD, *YOU Staying Young: The Owner's Manual for Extending Your Warranty.* New York: Free Press, 2007.

Schenck, Carlos H., MD, *Sleep: The Mysteries, the Problems, and the Solutions*. New York: Avery Press, 2007.

Smith, Jacqueline, *Animal Communication: Our Sacred Connection*. Lakeville, MN: Galde Press, 2005.

Tolle, Eckhart, *The Power of Now: A Guide to Spiritual Enlightenment*. Novato, CA: New World Library/Namaste Publishing, 1999.

Tolle, Eckhart, *A New Earth: Awakening to Your Life's Purpose*. New York: Dutton, 2005.

Walsch, Neale Donald, *What God Wants: A Compelling Answer to Humanity's Biggest Question*. New York: Atria Books, 2005.

Walsch, Neale Donald, *Conversations with God: An Uncommon Dialogue, Book 1*. New York: G.P. Putnam's Sons, 1996.

Zapf, Kim, *Wake Up to Your Intuitive Path*. Lambertville, MI: self-published, 2007.

ABOUT THE AUTHOR

Nanci L. Danison holds a BS Magna Cum Laude in biology, with a concentration in anatomy and physiology, a BA Magna Cum Laude in psychology, and a Doctorate in Jurisprudence. Until 1994, she was living the life of a successful trial lawyer in a large midwestern law firm. She often lectured on a national level and wrote on legal topics for the health care industry. Nanci at one time appeared on the Noon News for local TV stations in public service spots for the Bar Association, one of the activities that earned her a Jaycees' Ten Outstanding Citizens Award for community service. Then she had a near-death experience (NDE).

After her NDE, Nanci left the security of her big law firm and started a successful solo practice in health law, where she continues to be recognized for her legal abilities. Nanci's activities post-NDE include starting a local chapter of the International Association for Near-Death Studies, Inc.; earning a pilot's license in 2000, and Private Investigator's license in 2001; and sharing her NDE memories publicly. Nanci still practices law and writes books on what she remembers from her experiences in the Light. Contact her at www.BackwardsBooks.com.